Grammar Launch

Manabu Yoshihara
Chikako Nakagawa
Gregory Ashley

JN033979

KINSEIDO

Kinseido Publishing Co., Ltd.

3-21 Kanda Jimbo-cho, Chiyoda-ku,
Tokyo 101-0051, Japan

Copyright © 2020 by Manabu Yoshihara
　　　　　　　　Chikako Nakagawa
　　　　　　　　Gregory Ashley

*All rights reserved. No part of this publication may be
reproduced, stored in a retrieval system, or transmitted,
in any form or by any means, electronic, mechanical,
photocopying, recording or otherwise, without the prior
permission of the publisher.*

First published 2020 by Kinseido Publishing Co., Ltd.

Text design　　Medaka Studio
Illustrations　　Studio Bezel

 音声ファイル無料ダウンロード

http://www.kinsei-do.co.jp/download/4112

この教科書で 🎧 DL 00 の表示がある箇所の音声は、上記 URL または QR コードにて
無料でダウンロードできます。自習用音声としてご活用ください。

- ▶ PC からのダウンロードをお勧めします。スマートフォンなどでダウンロードされる場合は、
  ダウンロード前に「解凍アプリ」をインストールしてください。
- ▶ URL は、**検索ボックスではなくアドレスバー (URL 表示覧)** に入力してください。
- ▶ お使いのネットワーク環境によっては、ダウンロードできない場合があります。

◎ **CD 00**　左記の表示がある箇所の音声は、教室用 CD（Class Audio CD）に収録されています。

はじめに

　大学は、教室でクラスメイトとともに「英語を学び直す」最後のチャンスかもしれません。これまでも英語が好きだった人、英語に対して苦手意識があった人、大学には高校よりも幅広いタイプの学習者がいます。しかし、本テキストを手に取った人の目標は共通しています。

「英語上達の基礎となる『英文法』の知識を整理し、使えるようになること」

　基礎を固めることで、より高い成長が見込めるでしょう。本テキストは、基礎練習は「つまらない」、「辛い」という気持ちが先行しないよう、以下のように構成を工夫しています。

セクション	内容	目的
Main Points	Unit の目標を示す	「何ができるようになるか」を明確にする。
Preparation	英語の問いに対し、英語で答える。状況に合った表現を選ぶ。	現在の自分が英語で表現できること、できないことを認識する。状況に適した表現を「選択した理由」を説明できるかを考え、確認する。
Awakening	導入 リスニング	会話を理解し、その中で用いられている文法項目を確認する。
Grammar Part	文法の説明	Preparation で自分なりに表現した内容と、比較しながら Focal Point についての説明を理解する。
Exercise	文法を問う練習 練習は controlled/easy　→　less controlled/challenging となるように配置している。	さまざまな種類の練習を行うことで、ターゲットとなる文法事項を理解する。
Basic Phrases in Social Settings		日常生活の場面を想定して学んだことを応用する。
Final Touch		状況に応じて適切な表現を選び、それを選んだ理由を説明できるかどうかを確認する。
Wrap-Up Writing	Unit の前半・後半の総合練習	学習した知識を使って、会話、説明、意見、質問、プレゼンテーション等の文章を作成し、表現活動を行う。

　各ユニットは、上記の導入から練習までが2回行える構成になっており、前半が基礎的な文法情報、後半には、やや難易度の高い文法情報がくるように配置されています。さまざまな課題にチャレンジしながら、自由度の高い発言ができるようにステップアップしていきましょう。

　本テキストを使用したみなさんが、「できるようになった」という実感や自信をもてるようになることが、著者一同の願いです。

著者一同

目　　次

Unit 1

Simple Past and Past Progressive

過去単純形と過去進行形

Talking about the Past (1)

Main Points

- 過去に起きた出来事や経験を表す「〜した、〜だった」を表現する。
- 過去の習慣的な動作を表す「（以前は）〜した、〜だった」を表現する。

▶ **Preparation I**

Write or choose a suitable expression for each situation.

---

1. What time did you usually get up when you were a child?

---

2. You look somewhat different. と友人に言われた。

a. I went to the salon three days before.

b. I went to the salon three days ago.

c. I was going to the salon three days ago.

３日前に
美容院に行ったの。

BEFORE

AFTER

▶ Awakening I

A. Anne and Yoko are talking about what happened to Yoko this morning. Listen to their conversation and choose the best answer to each question.

🎧 DL 02　◎ CD 02

1. Where was Anne this morning?
    a. She was at college.
    b. She was on the way to college.
    c. She was at home.

2. What will Anne have in the middle of May?
    a. She will have a vocabulary test.
    b. She will turn in a report.
    c. She will have a meeting.

B. Listen to the conversation again and complete the sentences.

Yoko: Anne, where (1.　　　　　　) you this morning? (2.　　　　　　) my message?

Anne: I'm sorry I (3.　　　　　　) to your message. I (4.　　　) so sick that I couldn't get up this morning.

Yoko: How are you feeling now? Are you feeling better?

Anne: I think I'm OK now. I was just too tired. By the way, (5.　　　　　) something important?

Yoko: (6.　　　　　　). Guess what? We will have a vocabulary test in the middle of May.

▶ Grammar Part I　Simple Past

過去 単純形	• 過去において実際に起こったことを述べる。 • 一般動詞の過去単純形は、動詞の原形に -ed を付けるのが基本形。 　ただし、＜原形＞ go ＜過去形＞ went ＜過去分詞形＞ gone のように、不規則に変化するものある。日常でよく使われる基本動詞の多くは不規則形。

Focal Point 1: 過去に起こったことを報告・記述したり、過去における状態を記述したりする

相性の良い副詞：過去を明言する表現（yesterday, three days ago, in 2001, when I was young, last Friday など）

＜肯定文＞ 主語 + be 動詞／一般動詞の過去形 + その他の要素

I **missed** the first train this morning. [私は今朝始発電車を逃しました]

When I got here, **the place was** empty. [私がここに着いたとき、その場所は空っぽだった]

＜否定文＞ 主語 + be 動詞 + not + その他の要素／主語 + did not + 一般動詞（原形）+ その他の要素

I **was not [wasn't]** angry but disappointed. [私は怒っていたのでなく、失望したのです]

He **did not [didn't] take** the test last month. [彼は先月そのテストを受けなかった]

＜ YES/NO 疑問文＞ Be 動詞 + 主語 + その他の要素／ Did + 主語 + 一般動詞（原形）+ その他の要素

Were they easy to talk to? [彼らは話しやすかったですか]

—Yes, they **were**. / No, they **weren't**.

Did he **show** up at the party yesterday? [彼は昨日パーティーに来ましたか]

—Yes, he **did**. / No, he **didn't**.

＜疑問詞を使った疑問文＞

（主語を問う疑問文）疑問詞 + 動詞（過去形のまま）+ その他の要素

What happened to Kelly and Tom? [ケリーとトムに何があったの]

— They broke up. [別れたんだよ]

Who showed up at the party yesterday? [誰が昨日パーティーに来ましたか]

— Angela and Cindy showed up at the party. [アンジェラとシンディがパーティーに来ました]

（主語以外を問う疑問文）疑問詞 + be 動詞 + 主語 + その他の要素

How was the weather yesterday? — It was rainy. [昨日の天気はどうでしたか——雨でした]

疑問詞 + did + 主語 + 一般動詞（原形）+ その他の要素

Why did you **call** me last night? [なんで昨晩電話してきたの]

—Because I needed your help with my homework. [宿題を手伝ってもらいたかったんだよ]

Focal Point 2: 過去の習慣的な動作の記述する

相性の良い語句：always, usually, often, sometimes, rarely, never, every day など

My father <u>always</u> drove me to the station. [私の父親はいつも私を駅まで車で送ってくれました]

I went to high school by bike <u>every day</u>. [私は毎日、自転車で高校へ通いました]

▶ **Exercise I**

A. Put the Japanese sentences into English by filling in the missing information.

1. 今朝は何があったのですか？ ── カレンが寝坊して来なかったのです。

   What happened this morning? —Karen (   ) and (   ) show up.

2. 昨夜は何時に寝たのですか？ ── 私たちは午前3時までベッドに入りませんでした。

   What time (   ) to sleep last night? — We (   ) to bed until 3 a.m.

3. あなたはレポートを提出しましたか。 ──レポートのことをすっかり忘れていました。

   (   ) in your report? —I completely (   ) about it.

4. 昨日の旅行はどうでしたか？ ── ケンはとても疲れていましたが、アキコは疲れていませんでした。

   How (   ) the trip yesterday? —Ken (   ) very tired, but Akiko (   ).

5. 高校へはどのように行っていたのですか？ ── バスで通っていました。

   How (   ) to high school? —I (   ) to school by bus.

B. Listen to the recording and complete each sentence.   🎧 DL 03   ◎ CD 03

1. They finally (   ) a conclusion yesterday.

2. We (   ) in Kobe during Golden Week.

3. I (   ) last Friday night.

4. The group (   ), and they (   ) about 30 minutes late
   for the BBQ.

5. I (   ) a potluck party at my place (   ).

C. Listen to the conversation and answer the question.   🎧 DL 04   ◎ CD 04

What did Yoko do in Nagano during the spring vacation?

▶ Basic Phrases in Social Settings

A. Why were you absent from school yesterday? と聞かれて。

私は昨日熱がありました。

B. What did you do over the weekend? と聞かれて。

私は土曜日に買い物に行きました。

C. B のように、先週末何をしたのかをペアになって話しましょう。

① .

②

▶ Final Touch

Choose a suitable expression for each situation.

1. 「今朝、卵かけご飯を食べた」と、友人に言う。
   - (A) I was eating beaten raw egg poured on top of hot rice this morning.
   - (B) I ate beaten raw egg poured on top of hot rice this morning.
   - (C) I eat beaten raw egg poured on top of hot rice this morning.

2. 授業で難民について調べた。「彼らは自分の国に戻ることは一度もなかった」とプレゼンをする。
   - (A) They never got a chance to return to their home country.
   - (B) They hardly got a chance to return to their home country.
   - (C) They sometimes got a chance to return to their home country.

3. 不思議な設計の競技場を見て、「誰がこのスタジアムをデザインしたのですか」と聞く。
   - (A) Who designed this stadium?
   - (B) Did who design this stadium?
   - (C) Who was designed this stadium?

▶ Wrap-Up Writing

Using the dialogue below as a sample, make your own dialogue with your partner. Then, talk about what you did during your spring break or Golden Week.

Greg: Hi, Yoko. What's up? What did you do during the Golden Week holidays?

Yoko: I went to a dance festival. It was held in *Odaiba* for three days.

Greg: Really? I went to that festival, too.

Yoko: When did you go there?

Greg: I went there on the first day. I saw a couple of great dance performances. They were so cool.

Yoko: Actually, our team was on stage on the last day. You know what? We got first place. We won the whole competition!

Greg: Wow! Congratulations! I should have gone on the last day. Why didn't you tell me?

Talking about the Past (2)

Main Points

- 過去のある時点における進行中の動作を表す「（あの時は）〜していた」を表現する時制を学ぶ。
- 過去単純形と過去進行形を使い分ける。

▶ Preparation II

Write or choose a suitable expression for each situation.

1. What were you doing around ten last night?

2. Why was the game cancelled? と聞かれてサークルの先輩に説明する。

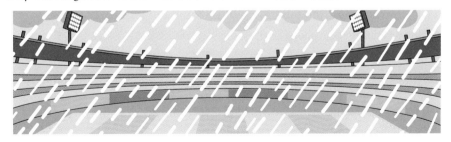

a. At that time, it rained heavily.

b. At that time, it was a lot of rain.

c. At that time, it was raining cats and dogs.

あの時、雨が激しく
降っていたんです

▶ Awakening II

A. Ken is asking about the girl Greg was with. Listen to their conversation and circle True (T) or False (F) for each statement. 🎧 DL 05 ◎ CD 05

1. T / F   Greg was walking on Ginza Street around seven alone.

2. T / F   Greg has a new girlfriend.

3. T / F   Greg's parents got married about 20 years ago.

B. Listen to the conversation again and complete the sentences.

Ken: Hi, Greg. (1.   ) on Ginza Street around seven last night with a girl? I'm curious. Is that your new girlfriend?

Greg: Around seven? Oh, that was my sister, Kate — not my girlfriend. Give me a break, Ken.

Ken: Your sister? OK. I trust you.

Greg: We (2.   ) to a restaurant to celebrate my parents' twentieth wedding anniversary.

Ken: Oh, 20 years! Please say congratulations to your parents for me.

▶ Grammar Part II   Past Progressive

過去進行形	• 過去のある時点で進行中の動作をリアルな感じで描写する。
	• 「あの時（その時）〜をしていた」という日本語に近い。
	• 過去進行形は、was/were + -ing の形で表す。

＜肯定文＞ 主語 + **was/were** + **-ing**（+ 過去のある時点を表す副詞）

I **was taking** a bath when the phone rang. [電話が鳴った時、私はお風呂に入っていました]

I found the book they **were looking** for. [私は、彼らが探していた本を見つけた]

＜否定文＞ 主語 + **was/were not** + **-ing**（+ 過去のある時点を表す副詞）

I **was not [wasn't] sleeping** then. I was thinking. [私はその時寝ていたわけでない。考えていました]

When Ms. Brook came in, the girls **weren't** studying.
　[ブルックさんが来たとき、彼女たちは勉強していなかった]

＜ YES/NO 疑問文＞ **Was/Were** + 主語 + **-ing**（+ 過去のある時点を表す副詞）

Was Ken **talking** on the phone when you came in?
　[あなたが入ってきたとき、ケンは電話をしていましたか]
　— Yes, he **was.** / No, he **wasn't.**

Were you **waiting** for the bus when I saw you? [私が見かけたとき、あなたはバスを待っていたのですか]

　— Yes, **I was.** / No, **I wasn't.**

<疑問詞を使った疑問文>

　(主語を問う疑問文) **疑問詞 + was/were + -ing+ その他の要素**

　Who was swimming in the river? [誰が川で泳いでいましたか]

　　— Shelly was swimming. [シェリーが泳いでいました]

　(主語以外を問う疑問文) **疑問詞 + was/were + 主語 + -ing+ その他の要素**

　What was he **singing?** [彼は何を歌っていましたか]

　　— He was singing *Yesterday Once More.* [イエスタデイ・ワンス・モアを歌っていました]

▶ Exercise II

A. Listen to the recording and complete each sentence.　　🎧 DL 06　◎ CD 06

1. She (　　　　　　　　　　　　) when you saw her.

2. They (　　　　　　　　　　　　　) in the cafeteria when you came to the office.

3. I (　　　　　　　　　　　　) when you called me. I (

　　　　　　　　　　　　).

4. **Yoko:** What (　　　　　　　　) Ken and Anne (　　　　　) at the entrance at that

　　　　 time?

　Greg: (　　　　　　　　　　　　　) to stop.

B. Yoko is explaining why she was late this morning. Use the words in the parentheses to complete the sentences with past progressive.

At 6:30 a.m., when I got up, my father and mother _____ (still, sleep), Emily, my younger sister, _____ (blow-dry) her hair, and my brother Brian _____ _____ (take a shower). While my sister and brother _____ (get ready), I was preparing breakfast. Before breakfast was ready, Emily left home for school. Then I had breakfast with my brother and my parents. I _____ (leave) for my college when Emily called me. She asked me to go to her high school to deliver what she had left at home.

C. Read the following instruction. Then listen to the recording and select the most appropriate answer.

🎧 DL 07　◎ CD 07

Instruction: Find the criminal who doesn't have a solid alibi.

A terrible crime was committed last night. Someone broke into a school at 10:00 p.m. and wrote something horrible on the board. Three people, John, Jane, and James, are suspected of committing this crime.

    a. John   b. Jane   c. James

▶ Basic Phrases in Social Settings

A. What were you doing while I was taking a nap? と弟に聞かれた。どうやら、おやつに買ったケーキが食べられていたらしい。疑われているのかな？

お前が寝ている間、自分の部屋で
宿題をしていたよ。

B. ハワイを旅行中に罰金を取られた話をしていたら、別の友人に「Why?」と聞かれた。

道路を横断中にスマホを
見ていたからだよ。

▶ **Final Touch**

A. Choose a suitable expression for each situation.

1. 「子供のころ、よく近くの川に泳ぎに行ったものだった」と過去を回想して、友人に言う。

   (A) When I was a child, I was often going swimming in the nearby river.

   (B) When I am a child, I often went swimming in the nearby river.

   (C) When I was a child, I often went swimming in the nearby river.

2. 探していた鍵を見つけた瞬間に「あった！」と、叫ぶ。

   (A) I find it!

   (B) I would find it!

   (C) I found it!

3. 「私がハリーを見たとき、彼は母親が迎えに来るのを待っているところでした」と、昨日の出来事を先生に伝える。

   (A) When I saw Harry, he was waiting for his mother to pick him up.

   (B) When I was seeing Harry, he waited for his mother to pick him up.

   (C) When I saw Harry, he waited for his mother to pick him up.

▶ **Wrap-Up Writing**

Describe what happened to you last night. Then compare it with your partner's description. Include the answers to the following questions in your description.

1. What were you doing at 7:00 p.m. yesterday?

2. What time did you start doing it, and how long did you do it for?

3. What did you do after you finished?

Unit 2 — Simple Present and Present Progressive

現在単純形と現在進行形

Talking about the Present (1)

Main Points

● 変化のない「真理や（科学的）事実」、あまり変化のない「日常の習慣的な行為」などを表す現在単純形を学ぶ。

● 動き・変化が見えない「物事の現在の状態や関係」、「心・体・頭の中の状態」などを表す現在単純形を学ぶ。

▶ Preparation I

Write or choose a suitable expression for each situation.

---

1. What do you usually eat for breakfast?

_____

_____

_____

---

2. 何かサークルに入った？と聞かれて。

　　私はテニスサークルに入っているよ

a. I'm belonging to a tennis club.

b. I belong to a tennis club.

c. I belonged to a tennis club.

▶ Awakening I

A. Anne is asking Ken about his part-time job. Listen to their conversation and choose the best answer to each question.

🎧 DL 08   ◎ CD 08

1. How many days does Ken work in a week?

     a. almost every day

     b. five days

     c. four days

2. How much money does Ken earn per hour?

     a. 1,100 yen

     b. 1,500 yen

     c. not mentioned

B. Listen to the conversation again and complete the sentences.

Anne: Ken, you have a part-time job, right? How often (1.   )?

Ken: I (2.   ) between Monday and Friday on the night shift at an *izakaya*. I usually serve customers and sometimes (3.   ).

Anne: Do you enjoy your job there?

Ken: Yes, I do. I (4.   ) around people and like helping them.

Anne: It sounds like you have a spirit of hospitality.

Ken: I guess you're right.

Anne: Ken, do you mind if I ask you your hourly wage? I'm looking for a job.

Ken: Sure. They (5.   ) per hour, plus my transportation fee. They also provide me with a meal each night I work.

Anne: Oh, you have a good part-time job!

▶ Grammar Part I | Simple Present

現在 単純形	①現在の習慣的な動作・反復的な出来事 　**相性の良い語句**：always, usually, often, sometimes, rarely, seldom, never ②現在を中心とした持続的な性質・状態。主に be 動詞や have，継続的な性質・状 　態を表す動詞，感情・知覚などを表す動詞（▶ p. 21 状態動詞） ③真理・社会通念・(科学的) 事実 • 主語が he, she, Tom などの三人称単数の場合、原形の語尾に -(e)s がつく。

<肯定文> **主語 + be 動詞／一般動詞の現在形 + その他の要素**

Lin usually **eats** buttered bread in the morning.［リンは朝はたいていバターをぬったパンを食べる］

My son **belongs** to the golf club.［私の息子はゴルフクラブに所属している］

Light from the sun **reaches** Earth in around 8 minutes.［太陽からの光は約 8 分で地球に届く］

<否定文> **主語 + be 動詞 + not + その他の要素／主語 + do/does not + 一般動詞（原形）+ その他
の要素**

I **don't drink** coffee at night.［私は夜に珈琲は飲みません］

She**'s not** a student at Harvard University.［彼女はハーバード大学の学生ではない］

< YES/NO 疑問文> **Be 動詞 + 主語 + その他の要素／ Do/Does + 主語 + 一般動詞（原形）+ その他の
要素**

Does Ken **study** marketing at university?［ケンは大学ではマーケティングを学んでいるのですか］

Are you **happy** with it?［それに満足していますか］

<疑問詞を使った疑問文>

（主語を問う疑問文）**疑問詞 + 動詞 + その他の要素**

Who always comes late?［誰がいつも遅れて来るのですか］

　— Helen always comes late. / Helen does.［ヘレンがいつも遅れてきます］

（主語以外を問う疑問文）

疑問詞 + be 動詞 + 主語 + その他の要素

How is the weather in Tokyo in July?［東京の 7 月の天気はどうですか］

　— It is very hot. The maximum temperature can reach nearly 40℃ on some days.

　　　［とても暑いです。最高気温が 40℃ 近くになる日もあります］

疑問詞 + do/does + 主語 + 一般動詞（原形）+ その他の要素

What time does your father usually leave for work?［あなたのお父さんは、いつも何時に仕事に行くの
　ですか］

　— My father usually leaves for work at 8:00 a.m.［父はいつも午前 8 時に仕事に行きます］

代表的な状態動詞

所有を表す動詞：possess, own, belong, have*

精神・心理状態を表す動詞：know, believe, imagine, want, realize, feel, doubt, need, understand, suppose, remember, prefer, forget, mean, think*

感情を表す動詞：love, hate, fear, mind, like, dislike, envy, care, appreciate

知覚を表す動詞：hear, taste*, see*, smell*, feel*

存在、状態を表す動詞：seem, consist of, owe, exist, contain, include, be*, look*, appear*

☞ have などの＊印が付いている動詞は、意味によっては進行形が可能です。

▶ Exercise I

A. Put the Japanese sentences into English by filling in the missing information.

1. トムはとても信頼できる人だと思います。

   I (　　　　　) Tom (　　　　　) a very reliable person.

2. 急いで。ぐずぐずしている時間はありません。

   Hurry up. We (　　　　　　　　　　　) to lose.

3. 終電は東京駅を午前 0 時 15 分に出発する。

   The last train (　　　　　　　　　　) at 12:15 a.m.

4. 私はふつうバイトが終わって 9 時頃に帰宅します。

   I (　　　　　　　) about nine o'clock after my part-time job ends.

5. コンサートは夕方 5 時に始まるのですか？

   (　　　　　) the concert (　　　　　　) at five o'clock in the evening?

B. Listen to the conversation and answer the question. 🎧 DL 09 ◎ CD 09

What does Yoko do when she has some spare time?

1. She often (　　　　　　) for her family.

2. She (　　　　　　) with her mother.

C. Listen to the conversation again and complete the sentences.

Mary: Hi, Yoko. What do you usually do in your spare time?

Yoko: I usually do a couple of things, but my classes are keeping me busy these days.

Mary: Well, when you **do** have some spare time, (1.   )?

※ <do/does/did+ 動詞の原形 > で、動詞の意味を強調

Yoko: I (2.   ), so when I can find enough time, I (3.   ) for my family. And my mom and I (4.   ). We (5.   ) on our drive and enjoy sitting and eating at an outside table if the weather is good.

Mary: That sounds relaxing.

Yoko: What do **you** usually do, Mary?

▶ Basic Phrases in Social Settings

A. How do you like your coffee? と聞かれて。

ブラックでお願いします。

B. 医師に What seems to be the matter? と聞かれて。

のどが痛くて、ひどく咳が出ます。

C. How do you like your coffee (or tea)? や How do you like your eggs? という質問に対して、自分の好みを説明しましょう。

▶ Wrap-Up Writing

What do you usually do in your spare time?

Sample ▶

   I usually do two things in my spare time. I like playing soccer, so when I can find enough time, I usually go to a park and enjoy playing it with my friends. And both my father and I like going camping. We put up a tent and enjoy fresh air and the sun all day long if the weather is good.

Talking about the Present (2)

Main Points

● 「今まさに起きていること、行っていること」を表す現在進行形を学ぶ。

● 現在単純形と現在進行形の違いを理解し、状況によって使い分ける。

▶ Preparation II

Write or choose a suitable expression for each situation.

1. What is she doing now?

_____

_____

2. 道を尋ねてきた観光客の人に言う。

私たちはここには住んでいません。訪ねてきているだけです。

a. We're not living here. We're just visiting.

b. We don't live here. We're just visiting.

c. We don't live here. We just visit.

▶ Awakening II

A. Greg is talking with Yoko on the phone. Listen to their conversation and circle True (T) or False (F) for each statement. 🎧 DL 10 ◎ CD 10

1. T / F   Yoko is with Anne in Shizuoka.

2. T / F   Greg is working at the beach.

3. T / F   Greg is going to join Yoko and Anne later today.

B. Listen to the conversation again and complete the sentences.

Greg: Hi, Yoko. It's me, Greg. What are you doing now?

Yoko: Guess what? (1.   ) on a beautiful beach in Shizuoka now. I'm sunbathing.

Greg: Ah, you told me that you were going there. I really envy you. Is Anne with you?

Yoko: Yes. We (2.   ) being lazy. How about you? What are you doing?

Greg: Don't ask. (3.   ) at the convenience store. I'm on my lunch break now. OK, Yoko, I'll let you go. Have fun!

Yoko: OK. Wait, Greg; Anne said she will have fun for you too!

▶ Grammar Part II | Present Progressive

現在 進行形	• 「今まさに起きていること、行っていること」を描写する。 • 「最近行っていること」、または「一時的に行っていること」を描写する。

＜肯定文＞ 主語 + **am/is/are** + **-ing** + その他の要素

    We **are waiting** in line to get into the movie theater. [映画館に入るために列に並んで待っています]

    Marie is usually calm, but she **is being** restless today.

      [マリエは普段落ち着いていますが、今日はそわそわしています]

＜否定文＞ 主語 + **am/is/are** + **not** + **-ing** + その他の要素

    He is **not lying** to you. He is telling you the truth. [彼は嘘をついていない。本当のことを言っているよ]

    All trains **are not running** due to the power outage. [停電が原因ですべての電車が走行していません]

＜ YES/NO 疑問文＞ **Am/Is/Are** + 主語 + **-ing** + その他の要素

    Are they **taking** a break now? [彼らは今休憩をとっていますか]

      — Yes, they **are.** / No, they **are not** (**aren't**).

    Is she **looking** for a new job? [今、彼女は新しい仕事を探しているのかな]

      — Yes, she **is.** / No, she **isn't.**

＜疑問詞を使った疑問文＞

    （主語を問う疑問文）**疑問詞** + **am/is/are** + **-ing** + その他の要素

    Who is working on this project? — I am. [誰がこのプロジェクトに取り組んでいるの——私です]

    （主語以外を問う疑問文）**疑問詞** + **am/is/are** + 主語 + **-ing** + その他の要素

    Which classes **are** you **taking**? — I'm taking the morning yoga classes. [どの授業を受けているの——午前のヨガを取っています]

    What are you **reading** these days? —I'm reading Keigo Higashino's new book. [この頃、何を読んでいるの——東野圭吾の新作だよ]

▶ Exercise II

A. Put the Japanese sentences into English by filling in the missing information.

1. なぜ電車が遅延しているのですか？　――強風のためです。

   Why (　　　　　　　　) this train (　　　　　　　　) late?　―― Because of the strong wind.

2. 彼らは、今ここに向かっていません。駅で私たちを待っています。

   They (　　　　　　　　) here now. They (　　　　　　　　) for us at the station.

3. 風邪をひきかけていると思います。[come down]

   I think I (　　　　　　　　) with a cold.

4. どうして彼がそんなにワガママにしているのか分からない。普段はそんなんじゃないのに。

   I can't understand why (　　　　　　　　) so selfish. He isn't usually like that.

5. 宿題やったの？　――いま、やっているところだよ！

   Did you do your homework?　― (　　　　　　　　) it now!

B. Greg just got a phone call from Yoko and is explaining what he is doing now. Listen to their conversation and complete the sentences.　🎧 DL 11　◎ CD 11

Yoko:　Hi, Greg. What are you doing now? Anne and I (1.　　　　　　　　) about you.

Greg:　I'm in a national park in the mountains with Ken and some other friends and we

　　　　(2.　　　　　　　　).

Yoko:　Oh, yeah. I just remembered that you told me about your camping plans.

Greg:　Well, now we (3.　　　　　　　　). I'm in charge of making curry.

Yoko:　Sounds nice! (4.　　　　　　　　)?

Greg:　Yes, we (5.　　　　　　　　), but I wish you and Anne were here with us.

C. Describe the picture using the present progressive tense.

have a picnic	a horse
sit, sit down	a duck
watch	two baby birds
run toward	a ball
run around	
play	
kick	the countryside
swim toward	the picnic blanket
wait for	football
shine	the ball on the hill

The Smiths: Dad, Mom, Kathy, and Will (…plus Skye, the dog)

▶ Basic Phrases in Social Settings

A. Have you seen Kentaro today? と友人に聞かれた。いつもと服装が違うから気が付かないのかな。ケンタロウなら、あそこに座っているよ…。

Kentaro is sitting over there. 普段は
ジーパンとＴシャツなのに、今日はスーツを着ているんだよ。

B. Where are you working? と母親に聞かれた。

I usually work at a hotel, but. . . 今日
は、ピザ屋でアルバイトをしているよ。

▶ Final Touch

Choose a suitable expression for each situation. There may be more than one correct answer.

1. 「彼らは夕食をカフェテリアで食べているところです。」と、サークルの先輩に説明する。
    (A) They have dinner at the cafeteria.
    (B) They are having dinner at the cafeteria.
    (C) They are eating dinner at the cafeteria.

2. 「天気が良ければ、たいてい私が犬を散歩に連れて行きます。」と、友人に言う。
    (A) I usually walk my dog if the weather is good.
    (B) I will probably walk my dog if the weather is good.
    (C) I am walking my dog if the weather is good.

3. 店員に May I help you? と挨拶されて、「（店内で）ただ見ているだけです」と答える。
    (A) I'm just looking, thank you.
    (B) I just look at it, thank you.
    (C) I'm looking for it, thank you.

▶ Wrap-Up Writing

Answer the following questions. Then write about yourself using that information.

What do you do?

What do you study at university?

What are you studying the most now? And why?

What did you do after school when you were a high school student?

What do you usually do after class?

Sample ▶

I'm a student at a university in Tokyo. I study Business Administration. Now, I'm studying English the most, because it is the language of business. I usually went to the city library after school to study when I was a high school student. After I entered university, I started working part-time, so I usually work four or five hours after my classes finish.

Present Perfect and Past Perfect

現在完了形と過去完了形

Talking about Experience (1)

Main Points

● 「過去から現在まで続く状態」、「現在までの経験」、「現時点で（ちょうど）完了したこと」を表す現在完了形を学ぶ。

● 過去のある時点から始まった動作が「ついさっき終わった」または「現在も続いている」ことを表す現在完了進行形を学ぶ。

▶ **Preparation I**

Write or choose a suitable expression for each situation.

1. Have you ever been abroad?

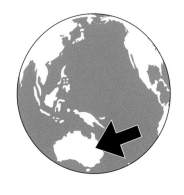

_____

_____

_____

2. 木曜日に「友人はどうしたの？」と聞かれて答える。

彼は今週ずっと風邪で休んでいます

a. He has been absent with a cold this week.

b. He was absent with a cold this week.

c. He is absent with a cold this week.

▶ Awakening I

A. Greg and Ken are talking about Tokyo DisneySea. Listen to their conversation and choose the best answer to each question. 🎧 DL 12   ◎ CD 12

1. Where has Greg been a couple times?
   a. Tokyo DisneySea
   b. Tokyo Disneyland
   c. both Tokyo DisneySea and Disneyland

2. What is true about Ken?
   a. He has never been to Tokyo DisneySea.
   b. He has been to Tokyo DisneySea only once.
   c He has been to Tokyo DisneySea a couple of times.

B. Listen to the conversation again and complete the sentences.

Ken: Greg, (1.   ) Tokyo DisneySea?

Greg: No, I haven't, but (2.   ) Tokyo Disneyland a couple times. How about you,

Ken? (3.   ) Tokyo DisneySea?

▶ Grammar Part I   Present Perfect and Present Perfect Progressive

現在 **完了形**	「過去」と「現在まで」をつなげて考える。 ①経験「今までに〜したことがある」を表す。 例文▶ 1, 4, 6 **相性の良い語句**：before, once, twice, three times, never, ever ②完了・結果「ちょうど〜した」、「すでに〜した」、「もう〜しましたか」、「まだ〜していません」、「（否定文で）まだ〜していない、（疑問文で）もう〜しましたか」を表す。 例文▶ 2, 5, 7 **相性の良い語句**：just, already, recently, lately, yet ③継続「…から今まで、ずっと〜が続いている」を表す。 例文▶ 3, 8, 9 **相性の良い語句**：how long 〜「どのぐらいの期間」, for 〜「〜の間」, since（+ S + V［過去単純形］）〜「〜（して）以来」

【注意】yesterday, 5 minutes ago, in 2012, when I was a high school student のように、明らかに過去を指す語句とともに用いることはできない。

＜肯定文＞ 主語 + **have/has** + **動詞（過去分詞形）** + その他の要素

1. I **have met** Ms. White <u>before</u>. ［私は以前ホワイトさんに会ったことがあります］

2. I **have** <u>just</u> **finished** writing an essay. ［私はちょうどエッセイを書き終えたところです］

3. They**'ve been** married <u>for</u> nearly fifty years. ［彼らが結婚して 50 年近く経ちます］

＜否定文＞ 主語 + **have/has+not/never** + **動詞（過去分詞形）** + その他の要素

4. I **have never worked** abroad. ［私は一度も海外で働いたことがありません］

5. I **have not finished** reading the book <u>yet</u>. ［私はまだその本を読み終えていない］

＜ YES/NO 疑問文＞ **Have/Has** + 主語 + **動詞（過去分詞形）** + その他の要素

6. **Has** she ever **traveled** abroad on business? ［彼女は今までに海外出張をしたことがありますか］
   Yes, she **has**. / No, never. / No, she **hasn't**.

7. **Have** you **packed** your suitcase (yet)? ［（もう）スーツケースに荷物を詰めましたか］
   Yes, I **have**. / No, not yet. / No, I **haven't**.

＜疑問詞を使った疑問文＞

【注意】When や What time...? のように「いつ〜しましたか？」を問う場合は過去単純形を使う。

（主語を問う疑問文）**疑問詞** + **have/has** + **動詞（過去分詞形）** + その他の要素

8. **Who has been** busy recently? ［誰が最近忙しかったのですか］

（主語以外を問う疑問文）**疑問詞** + **have/has** + 主語 + **動詞（過去分詞形）** + その他の要素

9. **Where have** you **been**? ［（今まで）どこにずっといたのですか］

現在 完了進行形	● 過去から現在まで続いている動作・出来事について「ずっと〜し続けている」ことを表す。主語 + **have/has+been** + **動詞（現在分詞形）** + その他の要素

I **have been waiting** for her for more than 30 minutes. ［30 分以上彼女を待ち続けている］

How long have you **been** reading the book? ［どのくらい、その本を読み続けているのですか］

—I **have been reading** it for three hours. ［3 時間読み続けています］

・直前に終了したことを表す。

Somebody **has been sleeping** on this sofa. ［誰かがこのソファーで寝ていた］

☞継続の期間を表す語句（for ten years など）を伴う場合、learn, live, sleep, stay, study, wait, work のように現在完了形と現在完了進行形の意味にほとんど違いがない動詞もある。

▶ Exercise I

A. Put the Japanese sentences into English by filling in the missing information.

1. 私はまだその本を買っていません。

   I (   ) the book (   ).

2. 彼女には、これまで一度も会ったことがありません。

   I (   ) her (   ).

3. 私の母は先週から風邪を引いています。

   My mother (   ) a cold (   ) last week.

4. 最近彼女に連絡をしましたか。

   (   ) her (   )?

5. マイクは10時間寝ています。そして今もまだ寝ています。

   Mike (   ) for ten hours, and he is still sleeping.

B. Listen to the recording and complete each sentence. 🎧 DL 13 ◎ CD 13

1. They (   ) the conclusion.

2. We (   ) each other (   ) we were kids.

3. My colleague (   ) him (   ) a long time.

4. She (   ) for about 30 minutes.

5. We (   ) since six this morning.

C. Kim and Greg are talking about health. After you listen, write the verbs in the correct form. 🎧 DL 14 ◎ CD 14

Kim: Greg, you look very tired. Are you OK?

Greg: I think I 1.   (be) OK, but I 2.   (sleep) well lately.

Kim: Is that right? How long 3.   (have) trouble sleeping?

Greg: For two weeks.

Kim: 4.   (see) a doctor about it?

Greg: Yes. I 5.   (go) to see a doctor yesterday. The doctor 6.   (say) I should eat well, do moderate exercise, and go to bed earlier.

▶ Basic Phrases in Social Settings

A. 生まれた場所と育った場所を聞かれて。

私は三重で生まれ、大阪で育ちました。

B. どのくらい大阪に住んでいるのかと聞かれて。

10歳のときから

私は10歳のときからここに住んでいます。

C. AとBを参考にして、自分が生まれた場所と育った場所を話しましょう。

Sample ▶

I was born in Ibaraki prefecture and moved to Saitama prefecture when I was eleven. I entered university in April 2020. I found an apartment in Kodaira city and have lived there since then.

▶ Wrap-Up Writing

Make "True or False" sentences based on your experiences.

Procedure:

1. Write two (or more) unusual or interesting things that have or have not happened to you in the past. At least one statement should be true/real, but others can be false/imagined.
2. Read out your sentences to the group.
3. The other students decide if they believe the statements or not and say "True" or "False".

Sample ▶

1. I have seen a bear in the wild.
2. I have been to more than 10 countries.

Talking about Experience (2)

Main Points

● 過去の基準点より以前に起きた出来事について「・・・（過去）の時には、すでに〜していた」
　を表す過去完了形を学ぶ。

● 過去進行形と過去完了進行形の違いを理解する。

▶ Preparation II

Write or choose a suitable expression for each situation.

---

1. Was Anne there when you arrived? と聞かれた Yoko が、次のように答えたい。

私がパーティーに到着したとき
には、帰ってしまっていました。

When I arrived at the party, _____.

---

2. 先週の金曜日に病院に行った理由を聞かれた。

それまで、しばらくの間あま
り体調が良くなかったの。

a. I haven't been feeling well for some time.

b. I hadn't been feeling well for some time.

c. I haven't felt well for some time.

▶ Awakening II

A. Greg and Yoko are talking about a reception party. Yoko had been looking forward to attending the party, but she couldn't enjoy it very much. Listen to their conversation and circle True (T) or False (F) for each statement. 🎧 DL 15　◎ CD 15

1.　T / F　When Yoko arrived at the party, a lot of guests had already arrived there.
2.　T / F　When Greg arrived at the party, Yoko had already eaten a lot of food.

B. Listen to the conversation again and complete the sentences.

Greg:　You got there late?

Yoko:　I mean. . . when I arrived at the party, it (1.　　　　　　　　　　　). And there were too many guests. . . . So, by the time we reached the food, most of it (2.　　　　　　　　　　　).

▶ Grammar Part II　Past Perfect and Past Perfect Progressive

過去 完了形	過去のある時点に視点を置き、「その時点」と「それ以前」をつなげて考える。 ▶過去のどの時点に視点が置かれているかを示す語句（過去形）：例）when we arrived at school, before I entered university, when they got married, I realized that ①経験「（ある時点より前に）〜したことがある」を表す。**例文▶** 1, 3, 5 ②完了・結果「（ある時点より前に）すでに〜していた」、「まだ〜していなかった」などを表す。**例文▶** 2, 5 ③継続「…から過去の時点まで、ずっと〜が続いていた」を表す。　**例文▶** 4, 6

＜肯定文＞ 主語 + **had** + 動詞（過去分詞形）+ その他の要素

　1.　I **had met** him before I entered college. ［大学に入る前に、彼に会ったことがある］

I had met him	＜過去＞I entered college	＜現在＞

＜否定文＞ 主語 + **had+not/never** + 動詞（過去分詞形）+ その他の要素

　2.　Although he **had not finished** his paper, he fell asleep. ［彼はレポートを終えていなかったのに、寝てしまった］

　3.　Kelly **had never spoken** to him before that time. ［ケリーはそれ以前に彼に話しかけた事がなかった］

＜ YES/NO 疑問文＞ **Had** + 主語 + 動詞（過去分詞形）+ その他の要素

4. **Had** they **known** each other for 20 years <u>when they got married?</u>

   ［結婚した時には知り合って 20 年経っていたのですか］

   — Yes, they **had**. /No, they **hadn't**.

＜疑問詞を使った疑問文＞

（主語を問う疑問文）**疑問詞** + **had** + **動詞（過去分詞形）** + その他の要素

5. **Who had already come** <u>when you arrived?</u>［あなたが着いた時誰がもう来ていましたか］

（主語以外を問う疑問文）**疑問詞** + **had** + **主語** + **動詞（過去分詞形）** + その他の要素

6. **Where had** he **been** <u>before he visited us in the U.S.?</u>

   ［アメリカの私達を訪ねる前、彼はどこにいたのですか］

過去	
完了進行形	• 過去のある時点まで、一定期間継続していた出来事について「…した時まで〜し続けていた」ことを、＜主語 + **had been -ing** + その他の要素＞の形で表す。

7. <u>By the time we arrived</u> at the hospital, Yoko **had been sleeping** for three hours.［私達が病院に到着したときには、ヨウコは 3 時間眠り続けていた］

▶ Exercise II

A. Listen to the recording and complete each sentence. 🎧 DL 16 ◎ CD 16

1. One of my friends (   ) my toy that my uncle (   ) for me.

2. The last train (   ) when we (   ) at the station.

3. Kate (   ) that she (   ) to write her name on the test.

4. We (   ) soccer for two hours when it (   ) to rain.

5. I (   ) forward to seeing her when I (   ) cancel the appointment.

B. Read each situation. Then complete the sentence that summarizes each situation by using the *past perfect* or *past perfect progressive* of the verbs.

1. John left the house at 7:30 yesterday. Mary rang John's doorbell at 8:15 yesterday.

   ▶ Mary _____ John's doorbell at 8:15 yesterday but John _____ the house.

2. I had arranged a business meeting. I arrived at the room and waited for the other members. After 20 minutes, I realized that I was in the wrong room.

   ▶ I _____ the other members for 20 minutes when I _____ that I was in the wrong room.

3. When I arrived at the party, Ken looked upset. I thought I had arrived there on time. When I looked at my watch, I realized that my watch was one hour slow.

   ▶ I _____ Ken waiting for one hour when I _____ the party. [keep]

   ▶ Ken _____ for me for one hour when I _____ the party.

C. Anne and Ken are talking about Ken's trip. After you listen, write the verbs in the correct form to complete each sentence.　🎧 DL 17　◎ CD 17

Anne:　How was your trip to L.A.?

Ken:　I _____ (not, go) to L.A. as I _____ (plan).

Anne:　What happened? I thought you were going.

Ken:　I _____ (realize) that my passport _____ (expire) only a few days before my departure.

Anne:　_____ you _____ (apply) for a new one yet?

Ken:　Yes. I _____ probably _____ (visit) L.A. during winter vacation.

▶ **Final Touch**

Choose a suitable expression for each situation. There may be more than one correct answer.

1. 母親が「起きた時には既に James が朝食を作り終えていたのよ。」と、家族に説明する。
    (A)　James had cooked breakfast when I got up.
    (B)　James cooked breakfast when I got up.
    (C)　James was cooking breakfast when I got up.

2. 「カナダに行く前に、英語を 6 年間ずっと学んでいた」と、友人に言う。
    (A)　I had been studying English for six years before I went to Canada.
    (B)　I had studied English for six years before I went to Canada.
    (C)　I studied English for six years before I was going to Canada.

3. 「どこにいて、何をしていたのかとケンに尋ねた」と、友人に説明する。
    (A)　I had asked Ken where he was and what he was doing.
    (B)　I had asked Ken where he had been and what he had been doing.
    (C)　I asked Ken where he had been and what he had been doing.

▶ Wrap-Up Writing

A. Read the following article. Then answer the questions.

   I had saved money for three years before I booked my trip to Spain in 2015. It was my graduation trip. Before my trip to Spain, I had never been out of Japan.

   When I went to Spain, I visited three cities: Madrid, Barcelona, and Seville. By the time I left Spain, I had toured many beautiful places. The church La Sagrada Familia was the most impressive site. I had never seen such a beautiful building before.

   I used public transportation while touring around Spain. Sometimes I got lost and asked for directions. I was able to ask for directions in Spanish. That wasn't hard because I had been studying Spanish for two years before I visited Spain. Before I entered college, I had never heard or spoken Spanish. I started learning the language because I became interested in Spain after I attended one lecture about it. On the day I left Spain, I realized that I had been speaking only in Spanish during my trip.

1. How long had the author saved money before he booked his trip to Spain?

2. Had the author heard or spoken Spanish before he entered college?

B. Write two more comprehension questions based on information in the article.

Future Expressions

未来表現

Talking about the Future (1)

Main Points

- 「意志表示」、「予定・計画」、「推量・予測」、「希望・願望」などを描写する未来表現を学ぶ。
- will と be going to の違いに気づくとともに、話し手の「確信の程度」に合わせた副詞の使い方を練習する。

▶ **Preparation I**

Write or choose a suitable expression for each situation.

---

1. Your father forgot to take an important document to a meeting.

私が届けるわ

Your mother said:

_____

---

2. 数日前から調子の悪い洗濯機を指して。

（このまま行けば）
もうすぐ壊れるわねぇ

a. It will break down pretty soon.

b. It is breaking down pretty soon.

c. It is going to break down pretty soon.

▶ Awakening I

A. Ken is asking Anne what she is doing. Listen to their conversation and choose the best answer to each question. 🎧DL 18　◎CD 18

1. What is Anne doing now?
    a. She is waiting for her friend at the gate.
    b. She is searching for a bike on the internet.
    c. She is having lunch alone.

2. What is Anne going to buy?
    a. a mountain bike
    b. a folding bike
    c. an electric bike

B. Listen to the conversation again and complete the sentences.

Ken: (1.　　　　　　　　　　　) buy a bike?

Anne: Yes. I have realized it's much cheaper and quicker to come to school by bike. I guess it (2.　　　　　　　　　) only 20 to 30 minutes by bike.

▶ Grammar Part I Compare *will* and *be going to*

未来表現	• 未来表現の will と be going to は通例、現在において話し手（書き手）がこれから先の事柄に関して述べるときに使われる。 • 単純に未来のことを推量する will に対し、be going to は、話し手が何かの前兆や兆しを認めて推量するときに使われる。

	will	be going to
基本形	主語 + will + 動詞原形 + その他 主語 + will not (won't) + 動詞原形 + その他 Will + 主語 + 動詞原形 + その他 疑問詞 + will（+ 主語）+ その他	主語 + be going to + 動詞原形 + その他 主語 + be not going to + 動詞原形 + その他 be 動詞 + 主語 + going to + 動詞原形 + その他 疑問詞 + be 動詞（+ 主語）+ going to + その他

	will	be going to
共通点	◆ Predictions これから起こることについての予測 I think it **will** rain tomorrow. I think it **will not** rain this afternoon.	◆ Predictions これから起こることについての予測 I think it **is going to** rain tomorrow. I think it **is not going to** rain this afternoon.
相違点	◆ Instant Decisions 状況に応じた即時の判断（意志決定） I'm thirsty. I think I **will** buy a drink. ◆ Offers or Promises 事前の調整とは無関係な自発的行為や約束 Your suitcase seems heavy, so I'**ll** help you carry it. I **will** call you when I arrive at the station. ◆ Requests 手助けや奉仕の要求 **Will** you help me move this table? **Will** you please come and see me tomorrow? ☞ please を主語の後や文尾につけると「依頼」の意味が明確になる ◆ Refusals (won't = will not) 拒絶「どうしても〜しようとしない」 I've tried everything, but my car **won't** start. He **won't** say anything to the police.	◆ Plans and Intentions 発話した時点より前から計画されていた予定・意志 We'**re going to** go shopping this weekend. ◆ Predictions based on Evidence/Signs 何らかの兆候や証拠に基づく予測 Look at those black clouds. I think it'**s going to** rain pretty soon. ☞ **Compare** A: Are you busy this evening? B: I haven't made any plans. I think I will **probably** watch TV. C: Yes, I'**m going to** see a movie with my friends.

Focal Point: will は、話し手（書き手）が持つ「今後それが起きる」という確信の程度が高いことを表す（100％程度）。will の後に probably（確信が 80％程度）を付けたり、文頭に maybe [perhaps]（確信が 50％程度）を付けたりして微調整する。

Humans will **possibly** live to 200 in the distant future.
COVID-19 pandemic will **undoubtedly** change the way people work.

▶ **Exercise I**

A. Circle the best word or phrase to complete each sentence.

1. (Maybe , Probably) I will call Ms. Smith tomorrow morning.
2. The party will (perhaps , probably) be held at the restaurant.
3. Anne, (will you , are you going to) marry me?
4. I got a job offer from a foreign company and I (will , am going to) visit their office next week.
5. I've tried to give her advice, but she (won't , is not going to) listen.
6. A: Look! There's smoke coming out of the machine.

    B: You turn it off and I (will , am going to) get the fire extinguisher*!

    * fire extinguisher（消火器）

7. A: Did you call Mr. Tanaka?

    B: I'm sorry. I completely* forgot. I (will / am going to) do it now.   *completely（完全に）

8. A: Your jeans are dirty.

    B: Yes, I know. I (will / am going to) wash them.

B. Yoko and Ken are having a conversation in Yoko's house. Complete the sentences with *will* or the correct form of *be going to* in combination with the words in parentheses.

Ken: When _____ [you, get] the result, Yoko?

Yoko: It's supposed to be this afternoon. Mr. Tanaka said that he would call me . . . but I can't wait!

[Yoko takes her smartphone out of her bag.]

Ken: _____ [you, call] Mr. Tanaka?

Yoko: Yes. He _____ [possibly, tell] me the result.

[The phone starts ringing.]

Yoko: It must be Mr. Tanaka! I _____ [answer] it! Hello?

[Yoko is talking on the phone.]

      . . .Thank you for calling. Have a nice day.

[Yoko hangs up the phone.]

Yoko: Yes! I was accepted to the program!

Ken: Oh, that's wonderful news! Congratulations!

▶ Basic Phrases in Social Settings

A. Will Ken come to the party tonight?
と聞かれて。

たぶん来ないでしょう。

B. What are you going to do this weekend? と聞かれて。

キャンプに行くつもりです。

C. 以下の会話を参考に、今週末何をするつもりなのかを、クラスメイトと話しましょう。

Sample ▶

Ken: Ken, what are you going to do this weekend?

Anne: I haven't made any plans. I think I will probably watch TV.

Ken: How about you, Anne?

Anne: I'm going to go shopping with my friends this weekend.

▶ Wrap-Up Writing

What is your friend going to do this weekend? Report your friend's plan.

Talking about the Future (2)

Main Points

● 現在進行形、現在形を用いる未来表現を学び、さまざまな状況での使い方を練習する。
● 未来の状況や条件について表す、副詞節（when〜など）を学ぶ。

▶ Preparation II

Write or choose a suitable expression for each situation.

---

1. Your grandfather and grandmother want to know about your school life.

夏に帰省した時にね

I'll tell you about my school life ....

---

2. 友人に予定を聞かれスマホでスケジュールをチェックしながら、家族と予約してあるレストランに行くことを話す。

今晩、家族と夕食に出かける
ことになっています

a. I am going out for dinner tonight with my family.

b. I will go out for dinner tonight with my family.

c. I am going to go out for dinner tonight with my family.

▶ Awakening II

A. Greg and Ken are talking about what they are doing tonight. Listen to their conversation and choose the best answer.   🎧 DL 19   ◎ CD 19

1. Who is going to buy a bike?
   a. Greg
   b. Ken
   c. Anne

2. Which of the following is true?
   a. Ken will contact Anne through LINE.
   b. Greg will give Anne a call.
   c. Anne will send a message to Ken.

B. Listen to the conversation again and complete the sentences.

Greg: Hey, Ken. What (1.   ) tonight?

Ken: (2.   ) to a bike shop with Anne.

Greg: A bike shop? (3.   ) buy a bike?

Ken: That's right.

Greg: Do you have any plans after that?

Ken: No, I'm free. Why?

Greg: I have three free gyoza coupons. (4.   ) to the Chinese restaurant. Of course, Anne can come along too.

Ken: Sounds good. I (5.   ) her a message on LINE now.

▶ Grammar Part II   More about Future Expressions

未来 表現	• 現在進行形は未来の確定している予定を表す。 • 現在単純形は変更できない予定・計画を表す。 •「条件」や「時」を表す副詞節の動詞の時制は、現在単純形になる。

be going to	What **are** you **going to** do this afternoon?
◆ What you have already decided to do or intend to do in the future. 事前に決定していた、またはするつもりであった予定。	— I **am going to** clean my room. Have you called Anne yet? — No, I'm **going to** call her tonight.
Present Progressive　現在進行形	What **are** you **doing** tonight?
◆ Specific or definite plans.　スケジュール帳に記載しているような、個人の決まっている予定。ただし、個人の都合によって変更もあり得る。	— We **are going** to the movies tonight. James **is coming** back from Hong Kong tomorrow. — **Are** you **meeting** him at the airport? Yes, so I'm **not working** tomorrow.
Simple Present　現在単純形	She **retires** next month.
◆ Scheduled events in the future.　時刻表やプログラム、アポイントメントのような、組織が決めた変更できない予定。arrive, be, begin, finish, leave などと一緒に使われることが多い。	Tomorrow **is** Sunday. What time **does** her flight arrive tomorrow? —Her flight **arrives** right at noon.
◆ Independent (conditional and temporal) clauses. 「条件」や「時」を表す副詞節で使われる。代表的な接続詞として if, when, after, before, until [till], as soon as などがある。	If she **comes**, I'll tell her all about it. It won't be long before the rain **stops**. I will give her my answer when I **see** her tomorrow.

Focal Point 1: 未来用法の場合、通例、未来を表す副詞（句）を伴う

現在進行形　I am having a party (now).［(今)、パーティーをしているところです］
未来用法　I am having a party tonight.［今晩、パーティーをします］

Focal Point 2: 相手の意向や希望を尋ねる表現 shall

助動詞 shall は「～だろう、～することになっている」を意味するが、現代英語ではあまり用いられない。
疑問文で用いる場合、「～しましょうか」を意味する。
Shall I open the window? (≒ Do you want me to open the window?)
Shall we go out for dinner tonight? (≒ Let's go out for dinner tonight.)

▶ **Exercise II**

A. Listen to the recording and complete each sentence.   🎧 DL 20   ◎ CD 20

1. (   ) anything special tonight?
2. My sister (   ) a wedding in Hawaii in December of next year.
3. What time (   )?
4. I (   ) as soon as I (   ) the hotel.
5. (   ) Mr. Tanaka, or (   )?

B. Complete each sentence by unscrambling the words. There is one incorrect/ unnecessary word or phrase in each.

1. もし誰かがあなたに電話をしてきたら、2時に戻ると伝えますね。
   If anyone calls you, I [tell, will tell, that, you, will be back, him or her] at two.

2. このレポートを終えたらすぐに、あなたに知らせます。
   Right after [finish, will finish, we, this report], we will let you know.

3. ＜タイムテーブルを見ながら＞　会議は午後 4 時 30 分に終わります。
   The [at 4:30 p.m., ends, is going to end, meeting].

C. Put the Japanese sentences into English by filling in the missing information.

1. あなたが明日ホテルに着いたら、電話を 1 本くれますか。
   (   ) me a call after (   ) at the hotel tomorrow?

2. （就職先が決まっているので）大学を卒業したら鹿児島に戻ることにしています。
   I (   ) to Kagoshima after graduating from college.

3. （時間割表を見て）スペイン語のクラスは 4 時 30 分に終わります。
   The Spanish class (   ) at 4:30.

4. もし来週の月曜日に時間があれば、それを持ってきます。
   If I (   ) next Monday, I (   ) to you.

5. 明日コーヒーでも飲みながらそのプランについて話し合いましょうか。
   (   ) talk about the plan over a cup of coffee tomorrow?

▶ **Final Touch**

A. Choose a suitable expression for each situation.

1. ゼミの教授に書類を忘れたと言われ、「(では私が) 取って来ます」と、教授に言う。
   - (A) I will get it.
   - (B) I am going to get it.
   - (C) I am getting it.

2. 「明日戻ってきたら、それに関してすべて話をします」と、彼女に言う。
   - (A) I will tell you all about it when I will get back tomorrow.
   - (B) I will tell you all about it when I get back tomorrow.
   - (C) I tell you all about it when I will get back tomorrow.

3. 「セールは明日で終わりです」と、客に伝える。
   - (A) The sale ends tomorrow.
   - (B) The sale is ending tomorrow.
   - (C) The sale is going to end tomorrow.

B. Read Ken's plan for summer vacation. Circle the correct expression to complete each sentence.

  I am planning to go to Yakushima in Kagoshima. It's a very beautiful and mysterious island. I've seen the movie "Princess Mononoke" many times. The forest on Yakushima was the inspiration for that movie.

  I am going to leave for Yakushima as soon as our summer vacation (will start, starts). I haven't decided how to get there though. Maybe I (will take, am taking) a ferry, a large passenger ship, which (is leaving, leaves) from Kagoshima port at 8:30 every morning. This trip (will be, is being) memorable for me.

▶ **Wrap-Up Writing**

Summer vacation is just around the corner. What are you going to do? If you have a specific plan for your summer vacation, write about it. If you don't have a plan, think about what you would like to do!

Modal Verbs (1)

Modal Verbs (1)

Main Points

- 「可能性」を表す can、「能力」を表す can や be able to などの助動詞を学び、状況に応じて使い分ける。
- 助動詞や時制による意味の違いを学び、「依頼」や「許可」を適切に表現する。

▶ **Preparation I**

Write or choose a suitable expression for each situation.

1. What would you say if you want to know the way to the nearest station?

_____

_____

_____

2. 自転車が壊れたことを知っている友人が、その後どうしたかを聞いてきた。

私は昨日自転車を自分で修理することできた

a. I was able to repair the bike by myself yesterday.

b. I could repair the bike by myself yesterday.

c. I was possible to repair the bike by myself yesterday.

▶ **Awakening**

A. Greg and Ken have just gotten off a long flight. Listen to their conversation and circle True (T) or False (F) for each statement. 🎧 DL 21 ◎ CD 21

1. T / F   Both Ken and Greg feel quite good after the flight.

2. T / F   Ken slept on the bus.

3. T / F   Ken will probably use Greg's pillow on the bus.

B. Listen to the conversation again and complete the sentences.

Greg: Yes, I (1.   ) some sleep. I feel quite good. How about you, Ken?

Ken: I (2.   ) at all. I feel tired. You know, I (3.   )

anywhere.

▶ **Grammar Part**   Modal Verbs - Ability and Requests

助動詞	• ＜主語 + 助動詞 + 動詞の原形＞が基本の形である。疑問文では＜助動詞 + 主語 + 動詞の原形＞となる。

can の用法

   a.〔能力・可能〕「～できる」

     I **can** be on campus early today.

     Money **cannot** buy everything.

       *can の否定形は can't や cannot を用いる。 2 単語 (can not) にしない。

     Can you swim?

     Yesterday was a clear day, so we **could** see Mt. Fuji from the Shinkansen.

       *see, hear, smell, remember, understand などの知覚・思考にかかわる動詞と用い 「（実際に）…できた」を表す。

   b.〔依頼・要請〕 「～してくれますか」

     Can you lend me 100 yen?

     Could you repeat that?

       ***Could** you ～? は 「～していただけませんか」 という丁寧な言い方。

   c.〔許可〕 「～してもよい」（*May I ～?よりも口語的）

     You **can** smoke outside if you want.

     Can I use a copier?

     Could I ask you a question? = I wonder if I **could** ask you a question.

       ***Could** I ～? は 「～してもよいでしょうか」 という意味で丁寧な言い方。

d.〔可能性〕 「～でありうる」

Such problems **can** occur at any time.

It **can** be difficult to concentrate on studying.

　　*could を用い 「ひょっとしたら～だ」を表すこともある。That **could** be true.

e.〔強い疑い・否定的な推量〕

　e-1 ［疑問文］「(いったい) どうして～か」

　　Can it be the best way?

　　How **could** she forget about it? It was only a couple of years ago.

　e-2 ［否定文で］「～であるはずがない」

　　Jim **can't** be ill. I just saw him playing basketball.

　e-3《can't + have + 過去分詞》［否定文で］「～したはずがない」

　　This **can't have** been a secret.

　　He **couldn't have** done such a thing.

be able to は can を使えない場合に用いる

① can は身に備わった能力を表し、be able to は一時的な能力を表す。

> 比較
> The baby **cannot** walk yet.
> Harry **isn't able to** walk because of his broken leg.

> 比較
> I **could** swim 200 meters when I was a hign school student.
> I **was able to** swim 200 meters yesterday.

　☞過去の１度の出来事で「実際に～することができた」は、was/were able to を使用することが多い。

② 他の助動詞や to 不定詞と使う場合や、完了形を表す場合は be able to を使用する。

I **should be able to** send you the documents by Friday.

I **want to be able to** play the piano.

I **haven't been able to** recall his name.

〔補足〕フォーマルな表現には be able to を使う。

　I am very sorry but I **am not able to** give you that information.

▶ Exercise

A. Rewrite the sentences using the new information in the brackets.

1. We cannot see the stars. [last night を加えて過去の表現に]

2. I can speak French fluently. [in two years を加えて未来の表現に]

3. Rina was able to visit Karen's home in time. [疑問文に]

B. Put the Japanese sentences into English. Use the correct form of *can* or *be able to*.

1. トムは永久に日本を去ってしまったのだから、昨日、あなたが見た男性が、彼のはずがないよ。

   Tom has left Japan for good. Thus, the man you saw yesterday (   ) him.

2. 夏でも山は比較的寒くなる可能性があることに気を付けてください。

   Please note that it (   ) relatively cold in the mountains even in summer.

3. 今朝は寝坊してしまったが、講義に出席することができた。

   Even though I got up late this morning, I (   ) the lecture.

4. 若いときは、辛い物を食べることができました（が、今はできません）。

   I (   ) spicy food when I was young

C. Listen to the recording and complete each sentence. 🎧 DL 22 ◉ CD 22

                                                                         Response

1. It's quite hot in this room. (   ) the window?   [   ]

2. (   ) that again, please?   [   ]

3. (   ) your ID, please?   [   ]

4. I (   ) give me a ride to the station.   [   ]

5. (   ) me with my homework this evening?   [   ]

D. Listen again and select the correct response to each request from the box below.

> a. No, not at all.   b. Here you are.   c. Sure, no problem.
> d. Of course. I was going to ask if you would like one.   e. Sorry. I have to work late.

▶ **Basic Phrases in Social Settings**

サークルの大先輩（OB）から，ホテルのフロントについたとの電話。出かける準備は出来ているので，ロビーに行くと伝えよう。

ロビーで待って頂いても構いませんか。すぐそこに行きます。

▶ Wrap-Up Writing

A. Read the passage and choose the best answer to each question.

The 2018 US Open women's final descended into chaos, with fans booing and play delayed before Naomi Osaka wrapped up the match for her first Grand Slam title. It must have been a great moment for Naomi, but there was no huge smile on her face.

During the ceremony on that night, the other finalist, Serena Williams, put an arm around Naomi's shoulder and told the crowd, which was still booing, that she was not satisfied with the result, but she would be able to overcome that. Then, she said that she would like the crowd to make the ceremony the best moment possible for Naomi.

On the ceremony stage, Naomi shed tears, addressed Serena's fans, and said the following: "I'm sorry. I know that everyone was cheering for her, and I'm sorry that it had to end like this. I just want to say thank you for watching the match. Thank you." She added: "It was always my dream to play Serena in the US Open finals, so I'm really glad that I (1. could / was able to) do that. I'm really grateful that I (2. could / was able to) play with you. Thank you."

1. Cricle True (T) or False (F) for each statement.
    (a) Serena was satisfied with the result.   T / F
    (b) Naomi gave a big smile during the ceremony.   T / F
    (c) Naomi had been dreaming of playing Serena before this match.   T / F

2. Which auxiliary verb is appropriate to use in (1) and (2) to complete each?

B. What do you think about Naomi's words at the ceremony? Write your opinion, and then exchange opinions with your partner. Try to use modal verbs when possible.

6 Modal Verbs (2)

Modal Verbs (2)

Main Points

● 「義務」・「推量」・「提案」・「助言・忠告」など、さまざまな意味を表す助動詞を学ぶ。

● 助動詞によって意図する意味の強さが異なる事を理解し、状況に応じて使い分ける。

▶ Preparation

Write or choose a suitable expression for each situation.

---

1. Ken doesn't like studying statistics, but he wants to be an economist. What should he do?

Your suggestion:

I think Ken _____

_____

in order to be an economist.

---

2. 一昨日、インフルエンザにかかった友人の看病をした。今日、自分自身も発熱…。病院で医師に伝えよう。

友人のインフルエンザがうつって
しまったに違いありません。

a. I had to catch the flu from my friend.

b. I may have caught the flu from my friend.

c. I must have caught the flu from my friend.

▶ Awakening

A. Ken is talking to Greg about a list that one of his family members gave to him. Listen to their conversation and choose the best answer to each question.

🎧 DL 23　◎ CD 23

1. Who made the list that Ken is talking about?
   a. His father did.
   b. His mother did.
   c. His brother did.

2. Which of the following is NOT Ken's job at home?
   a. Cleaning his own room once a week.
   b. Taking out the garbage.
   c. Washing the clothes he has worn.

B. Listen to the conversation again and complete the sentences.

Greg: Wow! There are quite a few things you (1.　　　　　　　).

Ken: Yeah, I (2.　　　　　　) my room once a week, take out the garbage, and wash the dishes I have used.

Greg: Since your mom said so, I guess you (3.　　　　　　) her rules.

▶ Grammar Part　Modal Verbs: Necessity and Prohibition

| 助動詞 | ・＜主語＋助動詞＋動詞の原形＞が基本の形である。
・過去の事について述べる場合は＜主語＋助動詞＋ **have** ＋動詞の過去分詞形＞となる。 |

<1>「義務・助言・忠告」「推量」を表す助動詞

must: ［義務］〜しなければならない、［推量］〜に違いない　☞主観的な判断（話者の意思）
　　否定形　must not, mustn't［禁止］〜してはならない

have to: ［義務］（規則や状況などから見て）〜しなければならない　☞客観的な事情
　　否定形　don't/doesn't have to［不必要］〜する必要がない

need to: ［義務］〜しなければならない　☞必要性がある
　　否定形　don't/doesn't need to［不必要］〜する必要がない

had better: ［助言・脅迫］〜すべきだ（さもないと…）（〜しないとまずい）　☞忠告
　　否定形　had better not［助言・忠告］〜べきでない

ought to:　［助言］〜すべきだ、…するのが当然（適切）である　☞客観的な意見、義務

　　否定形　ought not to［助言・忠告］〜べきでない

should:　［助言］〜すべきだ、あることがなされるべき　☞個人的な意見、助言

　　否定形　should not, should not［助言・忠告］〜すべきでない

can/could:　［助言］〜してもよい、［推量］〜かもしれない　☞可能

　　否定形　cannot, can't［助言］〜してはならない、［推量］〜のはずがない　☞不可能、不許可

may/might:　［助言］〜してもよい、［推量］〜かもしれない　☞支障がない

　　否定形　may not［助言］〜してはならない　☞不許可

<2>「提案」を表す柔らかい表現・丁寧な表現

- could や might のように過去形を使用する。（例）You could wear your red dress to the party.
- maybe, perhaps を最初に述べる。（例）Maybe you should socialize more.
- I think, I thought を最初に述べる。（例）I thought we might go to town and see a movie.
- (you/we) could always を使う。（例）We could always use olive oil instead of butter.
- probably を should の前後または ought to の前に使う。（例）You probably should offer your seat to them.
- might want to を使い丁寧な提案や助言を表す。（例）You might want to consider cycling.
- There's always を使う。（例）There's always tomorrow.
- It を主語にする。（例）It might be a good idea to tell your husband.

<3>「提案」を表すその他の表現

- Why not + 動詞の原形 〜？（例）Why not take a break at that café?
- Why don't you + 動詞の原形 〜？（例）Why don't you take some time out and rest?

▶ Exercise

A. Select the appropriate modal auxiliary verb to complete each sentence.

1. You (must / must have / have to) be tired after such a long trip.

2. Tomorrow is my girlfriend's birthday and I promised to give her something special, so I (might / have to / can) go shopping today.

3. You (mustn't / don't have to / cannot) go to Meg's birthday party, if you don't want to. You (need to / should / can) send her a gift.

4. I've heard that Henry caused an accident because he was talking on his phone while riding a bike. He (should / should have / must) been more careful.

5. I have called Ken on his landline many times, but there has been no answer. He (may / might have / cannot have) left his home.

B. Listen to the recording and complete each sentence.

🎧 DL 24　◎ CD 24

1. **A:** What (　　　　) I do?

   B: I (　　　　) you (　　　　　　　) wait until she has cooled down a little.

2. **A:** I (　　　　　) we (　　　　　) have lunch in that small café that we have just passed.

   We (　　　　　) have any other choice in this small town.

   B: Don't worry. (　　　　　　　) choice!

3. **A:** There (　　　　) be an easier way to deal with it.

   B: (　　　　　) we (　　　　　) ask for some advice from our professor.

4. **A:** (　　　　　　　) ask Jim to help you with those tasks?

   B: I (　　　　　　) do them myself and see how well I can do them.

C. Match the problems with the suggestions.

1. Anna's got an exam tomorrow.
2. I can't see well with these glasses.
3. Jim often loses his way when he visits Kyoto.

4. My father has gained weight.
5. Sandy has been feeling sick these days.
6. Sam messes around all the time and is quick to act goofy at school.

a. Why doesn't he go on a diet?
b. She might want to see a doctor.
c. She had better stop watching TV and start studying for it.
d. I think we should talk to him.
e. It might be a good idea to buy new glasses.
f. He should probably take a map with him.

▶ **Basic Phrases in Social Settings**

A. クラスメイトから Do you have time to join us for some coffee? と誘われた。行きたいな…でも、明日締切のレポートが終わっていない。

ごめんなさい、レポートを終えなければなりません。

B. ゼミでのミーティング。ゼミ長が11時開始を提案。早く始めて早く終わった方が良いな。

もし私が提案してよければ（If I may make a suggestion,）もう少し早く開始できるのではないでしょうか。

C. **What would you say if your friends invited you to tea or coffee ？ペアになって、A で 作成した会話をしてみよう。**

（例）Do you have time to join us for some coffee?
　　　　—I'd like to, but I have to babysit my little brother.

▶ Wrap-Up Writing

Some road signs in Japan are written in Japanese or different from the ones used in foreign countries. Tourists from overseas should be familiar with and be able to identify them. Explain some of the road signs in English.

This is a caution sign. The road (　　　　　) slippery.

This is a prohibition sign. Pedestrians (　　　　　　) cross the road.

This is a stop sign. Vehicles (　　　　) come to a full stop.

This is a direction indicator. You (　　　　　) go straight or turn left, but you (　　　　) turn right at the intersection.

Passive Voice

受動態

Passive Voice (1)

Main Points

- 「何かが（誰かによって）〜される」を描写する表現、受動態（受け身）を学ぶ。
- どのような場合に受動態（受け身）を使うのか、また、どのような場合に能動態を使うのか を理解し、状況に応じた使い方ができる。

▶ Preparation I

Write or choose a suitable expression for each situation.

---

1. 長距離バスで帰省したとき、Was the overnight express bus crowded? と聞かれた。

　　　　　　　　　　　ほとんどの座席は埋まっていたよ。

---

2. You look pale. Are you OK? と友人に聞かれた

　　　　先週の金曜日から頭痛に悩まされているの。

a. I've been bothered by a headache since last Friday.

b. I was bothered by a headache since last Friday.

c. I'm bothered by a headache since last Friday.

▶ Awakening I

A. Greg and Ken are talking about Ken's trip to Kyoto. Listen to their conversation and circle True (T) or False (F) for each statement. 🎧 DL 25 ⊚ CD 25

1.　T / F　　Greg is going to visit Kyoto next week with Ken.
2.　T / F　　Ken is staying in a hotel in Arashiyama.
3.　T / F　　Greg wants Ken to buy *namayatsuhashi* for him.

B. Listen to the conversation again and fill in the blanks.

Greg: When are you going to visit Kyoto?

Ken: Next week. I'm staying in a beautiful hotel near Kyoto Station. Originally, the hotel (1.　　　　) in the 19th century, but it (2.　　　　) recently.

Greg: Great. Is there any particular place you want to visit?

Ken: Yes. Arashiyama. It (3.　　　　) on the outskirts of Kyoto city and it is famous for its beautiful maple trees in autumn. We can enjoy colorful autumn leaves from a boat or train.

Greg: Oh, really? I'm so jealous. Well, Ken, as I've told you before, I really love *namayatsuhashi*. You understand what I'm saying?

▶ Grammar Part I　Passive Voice

受動態	• 受動態（受け身）とは、「何が（誰かによって）～される」こと、つまり「結果」を重視した表現である。他動詞に使われる。

受動態の基本形

能動態　主語（行為者）＋動詞＋目的語（被行為者）

Greg did all the work

グレッグが すべての仕事を 済ませた。

受動態　主語（被行為者）＋動詞＜ be ＋ done［過去分詞］＞（＋ by 行為者）

All the work was done by **Greg**.

すべての仕事が 済まされた **グレッグ**によって。

受動態の時制変化

	完了形	単純形	進行形
過去	The road had been repaired (before the mayor came).	The road was repaired.	The road was being repaired.
現在	The road has been repaired.	The road is repaired.	The road is being repaired.
未来	The road will have been repaired.	The road will be repaired (by next Monday).	不自然なので使われない

受動態の否定文・疑問文

否定文＜ be 動詞＋ not ＋過去分詞＞

The park **is not cleaned** by volunteers on Sundays. [その公園は日曜日にボランティアによって掃除されない]

☞準否定詞（never, hardly）も not と同じ位置で用いる。

Yes/No 疑問文＜ be 動詞＋主語＋過去分詞 ...? ＞

Is this park **cleaned** by volunteers on Sundays?

[この公園は日曜日にボランティアによって掃除されますか]

—Yes, it **is**. [はい、されます]

— No, it **is not**. / No, it **isn't**. [いいえ、されません]

疑問詞を使った疑問文

What is cleaned by those volunteers? [何があのボランティアによって掃除されるのですか]

Who(m) is the park cleaned by? または By whom is the park cleaned?

[誰によってその公園は掃除されますか]

受動態を使用するポイント

(1)「主役」が「〜される側」である場合

John had a tough commute to work today. While he was waiting for the bus, … に続ける場合、「主役」は John なので、a car almost ran over him（能動態）ではなく、he was almost run over by a car（受動態）が適切。

(2) 行為者が不明・（漠然とした）一般的な人・文脈から明らかである場合

The window **was** already **broken** when I came here. [私がここに来たとき、もう窓は割れていました]

English **is spoken** all over the world. [英語は世界中で話されています]

The newspaper **was delivered** at 5:00 a.m. [新聞は 5 時に配達された]

(3) 主語を表面に出さないで、客観的な記述をしたい場合

The bill for the repairs **has not been paid** yet. [その修理費はまだ支払われていません]

☞主語である you を出さず客観的に述べることで反感を回避している。

(4) 従節の主語を文の主語にした受動態の場合（it is … that の形をとる受動態）

People believe that the number <u>thirteen</u> is unlucky.［13 は縁起が悪いと信じられている］

→ **It is believed that** the number thirteen is unlucky. = The number thirteen **is believed to be** unlucky.

It is said that her GPA is 4.0. = Her GPA **is said to be** 4.0.

It is expected that the economy will grow by 3%. = The economy **is expected to grow** by 3%.

▶ Exercise I

A. Listen to the recording and complete each sentence.　🎧 DL 26　◎ CD 26

1. The package (　　　　　　　　　) to the wrong address.
2. Smoking (　　　　　　　) anywhere in this building.
3. (　　　　　　　) the first smartphone (　　　　)?
4. The meeting (　　　　　　　) until next Monday.
5. (　　　) that time heals all wounds.

B. Circle the best word or words to complete each sentence.

1. Pandas (is loved / are loved / love) by people around the world.
2. I (am / was / were) badly bitten by mosquitoes last night.
3. (Was / Is / Were) the film originally (release, releasing, released) in 1974?
4. The conference last Monday (wasn't holding / wasn't held / didn't hold) at the Hilton Hotel.
5. It (believed / believes / is believed) that the castle was built in the 17th century.

C. Put the Japanese sentences into English by filling in the missing information.

1. 電話はアレクサンダー・グラハム・ベルによって発明されました。[invent]
   The telephone (　　　　　　) Alexander Graham Bell.
2. どうしても、人はしばしば外見によって判断されます。[judge]
   Like it or not, people (　　) often (　　　　　) their appearance.
3. この映画はそれを観た人々によって特に推薦されています。[highly, recommend]
   This movie (　　　　　) those who have seen it.
4. 私の名前は会議中に出てきましたか。[mention]
   (　　　　　　　) during the meeting?
5. 私は誤解されたくありません。[misunderstand]
   I do not want to (　　　　) .

D. Listen to the message from Greg and complete the sentences. Then answer the question below in your own words.　　　　　　　　　　🎧DL 27　◎CD 27

Hi, Ken. One of the lanes on the main road (1.　　　　　　　　　　　　　　　　　　　　),
and I (2.　　　　　　　　　　　　　　). I (3.　　　　　　　　　　　) for the
party, so please start without me. OK?

　　Why is Greg going to be late for the party?
　　Because _____

▶ **Basic Phrases in Social Settings**

A. その本はいつ出版されたのかと聞かれて。

これは去年出版されました。

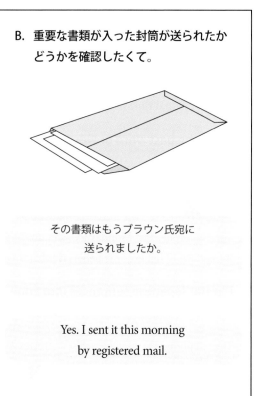

B. 重要な書類が入った封筒が送られたかどうかを確認したくて。

その書類はもうブラウン氏宛に
送られましたか。

Yes. I sent it this morning
by registered mail.

C. ペアになって、Bで作成した会話をしてみよう。

▶ Wrap-Up Writing

Yoko and Greg are talking about the school festival. Using the dialogue below as a sample, make your own dialogue about an event (a performance, sports competition, party, etc.) with your partner.

 ▶

Yoko: Greg, have you got any information on the school festival?

Greg: Yes, some.

Yoko: What do you know?

Greg: The festival this year will be held from October 30 to November 1.

Yoko: Anything else? Do you know who is coming?

Greg: Yes, a famous comedian will be invited on the first day.

Yoko: How about an artist? I mean a singer. Have they decided who will be invited to join our festival?

Greg: No, it hasn't been decided yet. The committee has approached a hip-hop group.

Yoko: Cool! It sounds like our festival is going to be a lot of fun. I can't wait!

Passive Voice (2)

Main Points

- 助動詞（can, may, have to, など）は、be 動詞の前に置かれる。
- by 以外の前置詞を用いる受動態がある。
- get + 過去分詞 〜で、「ある状態にある、〜された状態になる」という意味を表す。
- 受動態を使って、「依頼」や「被害」を表す。

▶ Preparation II

Write or choose a suitable expression for each situation.

---

1. What sports are you interested in?

---

2. 代表選手が試合後にインタビューに答えている。

　　チームメイトとうまくやれるか心配でした…

a. I was worried about whether I would be able to get along with my teammates.

b. I was worried by whether I would be able to get along with my teammates.

c. I was worried at whether I would be able to get along with my teammates.

▶ Awakening II

A. Ken and Greg are talking about Greg's parents' visit to Japan. Listen to their conversation and circle True (T) or False (F) for each statement. 🎧 DL 28   ◎ CD 28

1.　T / F　　Greg's parents are at Narita Airport now.

2.　T / F　　Greg arrived at Narita three hours late because of a traffic jam.

3.　T / F　　Greg's parents rested in a hotel for a while.

B. Listen to the conversation again and complete the sentences.

Ken:　Oh, Greg! You've been on my mind. Have your parents arrived yet?

Greg:　Yes, but their flight (1.　　　　　　　) due to a mechanical problem yesterday, and on top of that, their bus from Narita (2.　　　　　　　) rush-hour traffic. They arrived at their hotel three hours late.

Ken:　Oh, really? They must (3.　　　　　　　). Are they feeling better now?

Greg:　They seem to be OK now after unpacking and resting a bit.

Ken:　Where are you taking them today?

Greg:　We're visiting Ginza to see *kabuki*.

Ken:　Wow! They (4.　　　　　　　) seeing a live *kabuki* performance!

▶ Grammar Part II　More about Passive Voice

Focal Point 1:　助動詞（can, may, must, will など）は be 動詞の前に置かれ、＜助動詞 + be + 過去分詞＞となる。否定文は＜助動詞＋ not be ＋過去分詞＞

A new supermarket **will be built** here next year. ［新しいスーパーが来年ここに建設されるだろう］
The meeting **may be put off** till July 10. ［会議は 7 月 10 日まで延期されるかもしれません］
The project **has to be completed** this month. ［そのプロジェクトは今月完成されなければならない］

Focal Point 2:　get + *done*（過去分詞）～で、「ある状態になる、～された状態になる」という意味を表し、be + *done*（過去分詞）の形よりも動作性の強い表現になる。

We **got married** last year.［私たちは去年結婚しました］

The window **got broken** in yesterday's storm.［その窓は昨日の嵐で割れました］

You might **get hurt** if you stand there.［そこに立っていると、怪我をするかもしれませんよ］

Focal Point 3: 受動態の力を使って「依頼」や「被害」を表す。

① 誰かに依頼をして「物を〜してもらう」⇒　have [get] ＋ 物 ＋ *done*（過去分詞）〜

How much will it cost to **have the TV repaired?**［そのテレビを修理してもらうのにどのくらい費用がかかりますか］

Where can I **get my shoes repaired?**［どこで靴を直してもらうことができるでしょうか］

I **had my hair cut** yesterday.［昨日髪を切ってもらいました］

② 他者から被害を受けて「物を〜されてしまう」⇒　have ＋ 物 ＋ *done*（過去分詞）〜

She **had her bag stolen.**［彼女はかばんを盗まれました］

We **had our house broken into** last night.［私たちは昨夜空き巣に入られました］

Focal Point 4: by 以外の前置詞を用いる場合の受動態。

surprise のような「感情」や「心理状態」を表す他動詞の多くは、何かの影響を受けた心の状態を表すためよく受動態の形で使われます。その場合、文脈に合わせて by 以外の前置詞を伴う場合が多い。

His strange question **surprised** her.［彼の変な質問は彼女を驚かせました］

↓

She **was surprised at [by]** his strange question.［彼女は彼の変な質問にびっくりしました］

【by 以外の前置詞を用いるよく使われる受動態】

be amazed at 〜［〜に驚く］

be confused about 〜［〜について混乱した］

be disappointed at [by] 〜［〜にがっかりした］

be embarrassed about [at/by] 〜［〜に当惑した］

be excited about [at/by] 〜［〜に興奮した］

be interested in 〜［〜に興味がある］

be pleased with 〜［〜に喜んで］

be satisfied with 〜［〜に満足した］

be scared of 〜［〜におびえて］

be worried about 〜［〜を心配して］

▶ **Exercise II**

A. Listen to the recording and complete each sentence.

🎧 DL 29　◎ CD 29

1. Lunch (　　　　　) at 12:30.
2. This matter (　　　　　) secret.
3. We (　　　　　) a rainstorm on the way here.
4. I think we must (　　　　　　　) today.
5. I (　　　　　　　　) my lack of knowledge and language skills.

B. Put the Japanese sentences into English by filling in the missing information.

1. I was (　　　　　　　) of ghosts when I was a child.
   ［子どもの頃、お化けが怖かった］
2. I'd like to know if this project (　　　　　　) or not.
   ［このプロジェクトが継続されるか否かについて知りたいです］
3. Are you going to get your hair (　　　　　) tomorrow?
   ［あなたは明日髪を切ってもらうつもりですか］
4. Files (　　　　　　　) if the system suddenly crashes.
   ［もしシステムが急に停止するとファイルが失われる可能性があります］
5. A: Excuse me. (　　　　) this seat (　　　　　　)? ［すみません。この席は空いていますか］
   B: No, go ahead.

▶ **Basic Phrases in Social Settings**

A. How was the road trip? と車での旅行について聞かれた。 私たちは渋滞に 巻き込まれてしまいました。	B. How was the hotel? と、滞在したホテルの感想を聞かれた。 私たちは食事には満足しましたが、 サービスはひどかったです。

C. A と B の表現を参考に、最悪な旅の思い出をパートナーに伝えましょう。

▶ **Final Touch**

A. Choose a suitable expression for each situation. There may be more than one correct answer.

1. 「大丈夫です。怪我はしていません」と、ぶつけられた人に言う。
   - (A) I'm OK. I'm not hurt.
   - (B) I'm OK. I don't hurt.
   - (C) I'm OK. You don't hurt me.

2. 「見て！ここから富士山が見える」と、家族に言う。
   - (A) Look! Mt. Fuji can see from here.
   - (B) Look! Mt. Fuji can be seen from here.
   - (C) Look! We can see Mt. Fuji from here.

3. 「学校からここに来る途中で、にわか雨にあって、ずぶぬれになった」と、友人に言う。
   - (A) On my way from school, I met a shower and got drenched to the skin.
   - (B) On my way from school, I got caught in a shower and got drenched to the skin.
   - (C) On my way from school, a shower caught me and got drenched to the skin.

▶ **Wrap-Up Writing**

Using the script below as a sample, make your own presentation about a famous sightseeing site in Japan.

 Sample ▶

Good afternoon, everyone. I would like to share some information on the Statue of Liberty with you today. The tall green lady **is known** as a symbol of New York City, but it **was given** to the United States by France in 1886. Speaking of France, the Eiffel Tower and the Statue of Liberty **were designed** by the same person! The Statue of Liberty **is** sometimes **called** "Lady Liberty," and it **was placed** on a small island where it has welcomed many people to America. Small versions of the Statue of Liberty **have been constructed** in several other countries — including Japan.

Nouns and Prepositions

名詞・前置詞

Nouns and Prepositions (1)

Main Points

- 可算名詞と不可算名詞について学び、3 つの形（e.g., apple, an apple, apples）を使い分ける。
- 不定冠詞（a/an）と定冠詞（the）について学び、適切な場面で使い分ける。

▶ **Preparation I**

Write or choose a suitable expression for each situation.

1. What animal do you like the most?

I like _____ the most.

2. 警備員さんに入館許可証を見せなが
   ら言う。

私はこのイベントのスタッフです

a. I'm a staff of this event.

b. I'm a staff member of this event.

c. I'm staff of this event.

▶ **Awakening I**

A. Greg is talking with Yoko about some cats that his sister Lisa found yesterday. Listen to the conversation and choose the best answer to each question.

🎧 DL 30   ◎ CD 30

1. What happened yesterday?
    a. Lisa gave two kittens milk.
    b. Two kittens were given water and food.
    c. Lisa found the owner of two kittens.

2. What does Greg intend to do?
    a. He wants to have those cats at home.
    b. He's looking for a person who can keep cats.
    c. He doesn't want his sister to feed the cats.

B. Listen to the conversation again and complete the sentences.

Yoko: Yes, I (1.   ) very much. We (2.   ).

Greg: My sister Lisa (3.   ) in a park yesterday, and she took them home and (4.   ) and some food.

▶ **Grammar Part I** Countable and Uncountable

名詞の形 | ほとんどの名詞が可算と不可算の両方の機能を持っている。話し手・書き手がどのようなイメージでとらえているかによって、可算（単数形、複数形）・不可算が決まる。

☞ リンゴを例に、違いを考えよう
1) Put **an apple** in the bowl.
2) Put **some apples** in the bowl.
3) Put **some apple** in the bowl.

1) 可算の単数形（an apple）	2) 可算の複数形（apples）	3) 不可算の場合（apple）
a(n) は、全体から有形の個体を 1 つ取り出して示すときに使われる。	複数の個体が想定される場合は、「名詞 +s/es」の複数形になる。	形状の定まらない、例えば、料理用に細かくスライスされたリンゴ、または、すりおろしリンゴを指す。
☞ （どれでもいいので）ひとつのリンゴをボウルに入れてください。	☞ （どれでもいいので）いくつかのリンゴをボウルに入れてください。	すりおろしリンゴを指す。
		☞ すりおろしたリンゴをボウルに入れてください。

Focal Point 1: 「リンゴが好き」というように全体を指す場合には複数形で表す。 → I like apples.

数えられない名詞 （不可算名詞）
名詞を数えるか、数えないかは、「見え方、数え方」の問題。

1) 形状がない、または形状が小さすぎて、「数える」ことに関心が向かない物質名詞（液体・気体・粉末）

　　oxygen（酸素）water（水）rice（米）sand（砂）など

　　ただし、bean（豆）や pebble（小石）の大きさになると数えられる

2) wood（木材）や butter（バター）のように、切っても素材が変化しない物質名詞（原料・食料）

3) advice（助言）、nature（自然）や justice（正義）のように、形状がない抽象名詞

4) furniture（家具）や clothing（衣類）などのような、物の全体を表す集合名詞

Focal Point 2: 数えられない名詞の「数え方」……容器に入れる、形を変える。

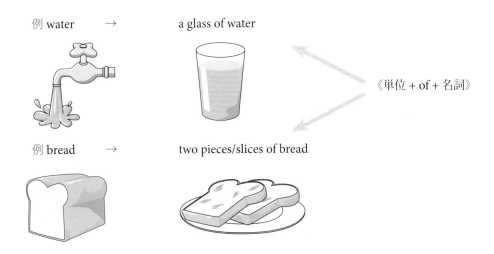

例 water　　→　　a glass of water

《単位 + of + 名詞》

例 bread　　→　　two pieces/slices of bread

☞ 他にも、by の後ろに続く交通手段（例 by car）や食事（例 dinner）や季節（例 summer）のような名詞も、通常は単数扱いになり冠詞がつかない。ただし、take a bus, take a taxi のような場合は、一台のバス、タクシーを利用するという視点から、冠詞 a が使われる。

☞ 表す意味によって、可算・不可算が変わる名詞がある。

1) I want **a room** of my own. ［私は自分の部屋が欲しい］

2) Our garage has **room** for three cars. ［私たちの車庫は車 3 台分のスペースがある］

▶ Deepen Your Understanding

不定冠詞　a/an	a/an は数えられる単数名詞に用いられ、（ある一つの）人や物、場所を表す
定冠詞　the	時に使われ、特定のものを指さない。一方、the は特定の名詞情報を表わす。

Focal Point :

- 一般的に季節を表す場合には the を付けないが、特定の年の季節を表したい場合には the を付ける。**The autumn** of 2019 was relatively hot.
- 最上級の形容詞、助数詞（first, second, third, etc.）、only、same、following などの形容詞が名詞を修飾し、名詞情報が絞り込まれ限定される場合。**Autumn** is **the best** season for hiking Mt. Takao.
- 常識的に、または話題としてすでに登場していて相手にもどれか・誰かが分かる場合。Excuse me, but could you tell me how I can get to **the station**? ※最寄駅が共通して頭に思い浮かぶ。
- 目や指などで指示することで相手にもどれか・誰かが分かる場合。
- 動植物、楽器、発明品などを総体的にとらえる場合。**The chimpanzee** is quite different from **the gorilla**. [チンパンジーはゴリラとかなり異なります]
- the + 形容詞で、「〜な人々」と総称的に（集合体として）とらえる場合。（例）the elderly「高齢者」、the rich「裕福な人々」。このときは、複数扱いになる。

▶ Exercise I

A. Listen to the recording and complete each sentence.　　🎧DL 31　◎CD 31

1. Could you help me move some (　　　　　　　) out of the room?
2. One group went by (　　　) and the other took (　　　).
3. The full English breakfast consists of (　　　　), (　　　　), mushrooms, and so on. It comes with (　　) or coffee and (　　　　) buttered toast.

B. Complete the sentences in each conversation.

1. **A:** Do you usually have lunch so late? It's already 1:30 p.m.
   B: 休日は、いつも 12 時ごろに昼食をとって、3 時ごろに果物を数切れ食べます。
   On my day off, I usually have (　　　) around noon and allow myself (　　　　　) fruit at about 3 p.m.

2. **A:** May I help you?
   B: 私たちはキャンプ用具を探しています。
   Yes, we are looking for (　　　　　　　).
   A: キャンプ用品売り場は 4 階です。エレベーターは右手後方にございます。
   The camping section is on the 4th floor. The (　　　　　) is straight back on your right.

3. **A:** すいません、このジーンズを試着しても良いですか。

Excuse me. Can I try on (   ) (   ), please?

    B: もちろんです。試着室はあちらです。

Sure. The fitting (   ) are over there.

C. Complete the sentences with the correct form of the words in parentheses. Add *the* if necessary.

1. She is considered to be one of (   ) of her generation. (fine pianist)

2. I would like to ask you for some (   ) on how to deal with the matter. (advice)

3. **A:** Excuse me. I'm looking for (   ). (city library)

    B: It is on (   ) of this street. (opposite side)

▶ Basic Phrases in Social Settings

A. 今夜は仲間と夕食。思い切って新しいメンバーも誘ってみよう。

今夜、私たちはご飯食べに行くんだけど、あなたもどうですか？

B. 夕食に誘われたけれど、今晩は無理。断るときは、言える範囲で理由も伝えよう。

そうしたいのですが、私は今、あまり現金を持っていません。2ドルしかありません。

あなた自身の言葉で…

▶ Wrap-Up Writing

Read the passage about the grizzly bear and complete the sentences.

Grizzly Bears

The grizzly bear (   ) the northwest of North America. It is one of (   )
in the world and weighs between 180kg and 550kg.

Did you know that the grizzly bear hibernates during winter? To do this, it must eat a lot during
summer and fall in preparation. It catches about 15 (   ) every day in the summertime.
Interestingly, it often eats only (   ) and eggs and leaves the rest for seagulls.

Another interesting (   ) about the grizzly bear is its family life. After mating, the
father leaves (   ), and so she has to take care of her cubs all by herself. She has to teach
them how to survive by demonstrating, for example, how to catch salmon and where to make a den.
(   ) that do not learn in nature's classroom won't survive.

ハイイログマは北アメリカの北西部に生息します。それは世界で最も大きな熊のひとつで、体重
は180キロから550キロになります。

あなたは、ハイイログマが冬の間冬眠するのを知っていましたか。冬眠するために、準備でハイ
イログマは、夏と秋の間たくさん食べなければなりません。ハイイログマは、夏の期間、毎日約15
匹のサーモンをつかまえます。面白いことに、ハイイログマはよく（1匹のサーモンの）頭と卵し
か食べません。残りの部分はカモメに残します。

ハイイログマに関するもう一つ興味深い点は家族の生活です。交尾後、父グマは母グマのもとを
離れます。なので、母グマは自分だけで子グマの面倒を見なければなりません。母グマは行動を示
すことで子グマに生き方を教えなければなりません。例えば、サーモンをどのようにつかまえるのか、
また巣穴をどこにつくるべきなのかを教えなければなりません。自然界という教室で学ばない子グ
マ達は生存できません。

Nouns and Prepositions (2)

Main Points

- There is. . . / There are. . . 構文を使い、場面を適切に描写することができる。
- 前置詞（prepositions）を使い、場所や時間について適切に描写することができる。

▶ Preparation II

Write or choose a suitable expression for each situation.

1. Describe the photograph.

2. できれば取り換えて欲しいので、お店の人に伝える。

すいません。スープの中に髪の毛が一本入っています。

- a. Excuse me. There is hair in my soup.
- b. Excuse me. There is a hair in my soup.
- c. Excuse me. There are hairs in my soup.

▶ Awakening II

A. Yoko and her father are talking with a real estate agent. Listen to their conversation and choose the best answer to each question. 🎧 DL 32 ◎ CD 32

1. Which of the following is NOT mentioned about the district?
   a. There are lots of restaurants.
   b. There are lots of department stores.
   c. There is a lot of beautiful nature.

2. Which of the following is a bad point about the apartment?

    a.   Some neighbors are not friendly.

    b.   The rooms are okay but without a view of the lake.

    c.   The rent is expensive.

B. Listen to the conversation again and complete the sentences.

Yoko: (1.   ) any stores near here?

Agent: Sure. (2.   ) a grocery store (3.   ) the apartment.

▶ **Grammar Part II** *There is, There are* and Prepositions

In the Neighborhood (N):

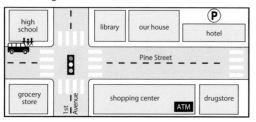

At home (H):

in　空間的な広がりのある環境の中にいる *H:* There are a sofa and two armchairs **in** the room. *H:* There is plenty of water **in** the vase.	at　ある一点で接している *N:* Our high school is located **at** the intersection of Pine Street and 1st Avenue. *H:* There is a school bus that arrives **at** 9:00.
on (on top of)　平面的な部分に接触している *H:* There is a clock **on** the wall. *H:* There is a vase **on**/**on top of** the bookshelf.	under　あるものの下にある *H:* There is a cat **under** the table.
below　基準よりも低いところにある *H:* There is a telephone **below** the picture.	above　基準よりも高いところにある *H:* There is a picture **above** the telephone.
inside　内側にいる *N:* There is an ATM **inside** the shopping center.	outside　外側にいる *H:* There are two children **outside** the house.

between　２つのものに挟まれている
N: Our house is located **between** the library and the
    hotel.
	among　３つ以上の何かに取り囲まれている
	H: There is a small table **among** the sofa and the
	    armchairs.

near　対象とそう遠くない近い位置にある *N:* The library is located **near** the hotel.	next to　対象と隣り合った位置にある *N:* The library is located **next to** our house.
by　すぐそばに近接している *H:* Is there a telephone **by** the window?	beside　対象のかたわらに並んでいる *H:* Are there any cats **beside** the TV?
behind　何かの後ろに隠れる *N:* There is a parking lot **behind** the hotel. *H:* There is a cat **behind** the sofa.	in front of　何かの前にある *N:* There is a bus **in front of** our house. *H:* There is a man **in front of** the woman at the door.

Focal Point 1: There be 動詞 + subject + place/time で、「何か新しい物」「知らない誰か」の存在を表す。

- There is + a/an 可算名詞（単数）+ 場所 / 時間を表す表現
  There is a bridge over the river.［川に橋が架かっています］
- There are + 可算名詞（複数）+ 場所 / 時間を表す表現
  There are two children outside the house.［家の外に子どもが二人います］
- There is + 不可算名詞 + 場所／時間を表す表現
  There is very little water in the bucket.［そのバケツにはほとんど水が入っていません］

Focal Point 2: Be 動詞 + there + (any) subject + place/time で、Yes/No の疑問文になる。

- Is there is + a/an 可算名詞（単数）+ 場所 / 時間を表す表現
  Is there a telephone by the window?［窓のそばに電話がありますか］
  — Yes, **there is**.［はい、あります］／ No, **there isn't**.［いいえ、ありません］
- Are there + (any) 可算名詞（複数）+ 場所 / 時間を表す表現
  Are there any cats near the TV?［テレビの近くに猫がいますか］
  — Yes, **there are**.［はい、います］／ No, **there aren't**.［いいえ、いません］
- Is there + (any) 不可算名詞 + 場所／時間を表す表現
  Is there any water in the vase?［その花瓶に水が入っていますか］
  — Yes, **there is**.［はい、入っています］／ No, **there isn't**.［いいえ、入っていません］

Focal Point 3: There be 動詞 + not + (any) subject + place/time で、否定文になる。

- There is + not + a/an 可算名詞（単数）+ 場所／時間を表す表現
  There is not a suitcase under the bed.［ベッドの下にスーツケースは一つもありません］
- There are + not + (any) 可算名詞（複数）+ 場所／時間を表す表現
  There are not any clouds over the mountain.［山に雲はかかっていません］
- There is + not + (any) 不可算名詞 + 場所／時間を表す表現
  There is not any water in the glass.［そのコップには水が入っていません］

▶ **Exercise II**

A. Describe the picture using the correct form of the noun in parentheses (a/an/the – or other counting word – five, several, etc.) and add an appropriate preposition.

1. There are (   ) the tall wooden stand.   (goat)
2. There is (   ) the fence.   (woman)
3. There are (   ) the fence.   (tree)

B. You and your friends are going to cook curry and rice at a campsite. What do you need to buy? Ask your partner to check what you already have.

Ingredients (4 servings)

200g of beef   3 onions   2 carrots
3 potatoes 1 tablespoon of oil
1 box of curry sauce mix   450g of rice

Yes/No Questions	Answers
1. Is there enough beef in the refrigerator?	No. .
2. Are there any onions in the kitchen?	Yes, there .
3. How many carrots are there in the refrigerator?	There .
4. Are there any potatoes in the refrigerator?	Yes, there .
5. Is there any oil in the kitchen?	Yes, there of oil.
6. Is there a box of curry sauce mix in the kitchen?	.
7. Is there any rice in the kitchen?	Yes, there of rice.

C. Make a shopping list before you go shopping.

▶ Final Touch

A. Choose a suitable expression for each situation. There may be more than one correct answer.

1. 多くの人が搭乗している飛行機で「お医者さまはいらっしゃいますか」というアナウンスをする。

   (A)   Are there doctors on board?

   (B)   Is there a doctor between the passengers?

   (C)   Is there a doctor on the airplane?

2. 映画鑑賞をするために集まった友人に、「プロジェクターは天井にあって、電源は壁についているよ」と言う。

   (A)   The projector is on the ceiling and its power switch is on the wall.

   (B)   The projector is under the ceiling and its power switch is by the wall.

   (C)   The projector is below the ceiling and its power switch is next to the wall.

3. 「車のトランクにもう一つ荷物を積める空間がある」と、友人に言う。

   (A)   There is a room in the trunk for one more piece of luggage.

   (B)   There is room in the trunk for one more piece of luggage.

   (C)   There are rooms in the trunk for one more luggage.

▶ Wrap-Up Writing

1. Read the paragraph below. What is in the place the author describes.

My favorite town

I like Kichijoji because it is surrounded by beautiful nature. There is a large park near the main station. We can find many nice restaurants and cafés along the street to the park. There is a zoo and a small aquarium, and some playgrounds in the park. Thus, there are always a lot of children and their parents in Kichijoji. There is a large lake in the center of the park. We can rent a small boat there. Because there is no free parking, it would be better to visit Kichijoji by train.

2. Write about a place you like. Use the paragraph above to help you.

Unit 9 — Infinitives and Gerunds

不定詞・動名詞

Infinitives and Gerunds (1)

Main Points

- 不定詞 <to + *do*（動詞の原形）> が持つ３つの用法を学ぶ。
  ①動詞を修飾する副詞的用法、②名詞を修飾する形容詞的用法、③名詞の機能を果たす名詞的用法

▶ **Preparation I**

Write or choose a suitable expression for each situation.

1. What are the purposes of your studying at college?

   I study at college in order …

2. Are you available tonight? We are holding a birthday party for Marie. と パーティーに誘われた。

   ごめん行けないや。終わらせなければなら ない課題があるから。

   I'm sorry I can't make it.

   a. I have an assignment to finish today.
   b. My assignment is finishing today.
   c. My assignment is to finish today.

▶ Awakening I

A. Greg and Yoko are talking about a camping trip. Listen to their conversation and choose the best answer to each question. 🎧 DL 33 ◎ CD 33

1. When will they go camping?
   a. early September
   b. late October
   c. early November

2. Who does Yoko want to invite to go camping?
   a. It's Bob.
   b. It's Takeshi.
   c. It's Ken.

B. Listen to the conversation again and complete the sentences.

Greg: Hey, Yoko. Do you have a minute?

Yoko: Sure. What is it?

Greg: I'm (1.   ) in Hakone (2.   ) the beautiful autumn leaves.

Yoko: Sounds good. I (3.   ) with you. When are you going?

Greg: In early November. I think it's (4.   ) the area, right?

Yoko: I think you're right. Who else is coming?

Greg: Well, Bob, Takeshi, Akiko, and Anne.

Yoko: How about Ken? Can I invite him, too?

Greg: Sure. I will be (5.   ). He is a good cook.

▶ Grammar Part I Infinitives and Gerunds

- 不定詞＜ to *do*（動詞の原形）＞の 3 つの用法：①副詞的用法、②形容詞的用法、③名詞的用法

Focal Point 1: 副詞的用法は、①動詞が示す行為の目的、②原因、③結果を表す。

① **目的** I went to the library yesterday **to return** the books.［本を返すために昨日図書館に行きました］
   I got up early this morning **to watch** a soccer game.
   ［サッカーの試合を観るために今朝早く起きました］
   in order to や so as to の形でも使われる。

② 原因　I was glad **to receive** a letter from her.［彼女から手紙を受け取って嬉しかった］

My father was surprised **to hear** the news.［父はその知らせを聞いて驚いた］

根拠　He must be rich **to buy** such a car.［あんな車を買うなんて金持ちに違いない］

③ 結果　He has grown up **to be** a famous soccer player.

［彼は成長して有名なサッカー選手になりました］

I arrived at the station, **only to** find that train had already left.［駅に到着したが、結局は電車がすでに出ていたのが分かっただけでした］

She left Japan, **never to** return.［彼女は日本を出て、二度と戻って来ませんでした］

☞ only *to do*「結局〜しただけ」、never *to do*「二度と〜しなかった」という意味。

Focal Point 2:　名詞を修飾する形容詞的用法は、「〜するための…」、「〜すべき…」という意味で、名詞の直後に置かれ、目的・用途を説明する。

Would you like something　**to drink?**［何か飲み物いかがですか］

There are many things **to do** tomorrow.［明日すべきことがたくさんあります］

Focal Point 3:　名詞的用法は、①動詞の目的語、② be 動詞の補語、③主語を表す。

① **動詞の目的語「〜することを」**

My father decided **to quit** smoking.［私の父はタバコをやめることを決心しました］

☞否定形は **not** *to do* となる。I promise **not to tell** lies.［嘘は言わないと約束します］

② **be 動詞の補語「〜することだ」**

The only solution was **to try** again.［唯一の解決策は再挑戦することであった］

☞ All の後に関係代名詞 that が省略された All you have to do is などを主語とし、be 動詞の前に to do がある場合には、be 動詞の後に動詞の原形を続ける。

All you have to do is **(to) click** the link.［リンクをクリックしさえすればいいですよ］

③ **主語「〜することは」**

To swim in that sea is dangerous.［あの海で泳ぐことは危険だ］

= **It** is dangerous **to swim** in that sea. 不定詞（to swim）の主語が「一般の人」の場合は意味上の主語は示さない。

☞意味上の主語を表す場合＜ for A+ to do ＞

It is dangerous **for children** to swim in that sea.［子どもがあの海で泳ぐことは危険だ］

人物評価を表す形容詞の場合には＜ of A + to do ＞

It is kind **of you** to show me around this city.［街を案内してくれるなんてあなたは親切だ］

☞形式主語 it を用いることが一般的な動詞には be 動詞，cost, seem, take などがある。

It costs five thousand dollars **to buy** this car.［この車を買うのに 5000 ドルかかる］

It seems difficult **to get** good results in short time.［短期間で良い結果を得るのは難しいだろう］

▶ **Exercise I**

A. Listen to the recording and complete each sentence.   🎧 DL 34   ◎ CD 34

1. We should arrive early (   ).

2. I've got (   ).

3. It (   ) to leave the door unlocked.

4. The main aim of this intensive course (   ) your writing.

5. It took him a while (   ) to his new surroundings.

B. Match the sentences.

1. Why did you go to the library yesterday?   [   ]

2. I've heard Yoko didn't pass the driving test.   [   ]

3. What should I do, Anne? I'm nervous.   [   ]

4. Ken, I don't want to talk about it now.   [   ]

5. Are you going somewhere during winter vacation?   [   ]

    a.   All you can do now is wait and hope.

    b.   Yes, I've decided to go back to my hometown.

    c.   Yoko, please give me a chance to explain.

    d.   To return the books I borrowed.

    e.   Oh, really? I'm sorry to hear that.

C. Complete each conversation. Put the Japanese sentence into English by filling in the missing information.

1. **A:** Nancy, do you (   ) us for some coffee?
    ナンシー、コーヒーを一緒に飲む時間はありますか。
    B: I'm sorry, but I can't. I have to do my laundry.

2. **A:** How long did it take to come here from your campus?
    B: It (   ) to come here by bus.
    ここまでバスで約 20 分かかりました。

3. **A:** Hey, Bob. I haven't seen you in ages.
    B: Greg! It's good (   )! It has been five years, right?
    グレッグ！また会えてうれしいよ。5 年ぶりだよね。

4. **A:** Would you like (   ) to my place (   ) a football game tonight?
    サッカーの試合を見るために、今晩私のところへ来ませんか。
    B: That sounds great! Would you like me to bring (   )?
    いいね！何か食べ物を持って行きましょうか。
    A: No, you don't have to. Just bring yourself.

▶ Basic Phrases in Social Settings

A. 子どもの頃の夢は何だったかと聞かれて。

私の夢は、パイロットになることでした。

B. How long does it take to come to campus from your home?

It takes . . . to 〜 here by/on

▶ Wrap-Up Writng

Using the dialogue below as a sample, make your own dialogue with your partner.

Yoko wants Greg to check her computer.

Yoko: Hi, Greg! Come in. Thank you for coming over.

Greg: Sure. It's my pleasure.

Yoko: Greg, would you like something to drink?

Greg: Yes, coffee, please, if you have some. So, Yoko, what would you like me to do today?

Yoko: Well, something is wrong with my computer. You are an expert in computers, right? I need you to fix it today if possible. I have a very important report to write by tomorrow.

Greg: OK. Let me take a look at it. While working on it, I don't mind you using my computer to start your report.

Yoko: Thank you! That would really help me out.

Infinitives and Gerunds (2)

Main Points

● 動詞が名詞化された「動名詞」の用法を学ぶ。
● 動名詞と不定詞を使い分ける。

▶ Preparation II

Write or choose a suitable expression for each situation.

<table>
<tr>
<td>

1. How shall we get to the Musashi-murayama campus? と聞かれて、国分寺キャンパスからバスで行くことを提案したい。

</td>
<td>

2. Did you enjoy your time here? と聞かれて。

a. Yes! I will never forget visiting this country.
b. Yes! I will never forget to visit this country.
c. Yes! I will remember to visit this country.

</td>
</tr>
</table>

▶ Awakening II

A. Yoko and Anne are talking about going out this evening. Listen to the conversation and complete the sentences.　　　　　　　　🎧 DL 35　◎ CD 35

Yoko: Hey, Anne. I (1.　　　　　　　　　　　　) this evening.

Anne: OK. What do you want to do?

Yoko: (2.　　　　　　　　　　) to karaoke (3.　　　　　　　　　　)?

Anne: Sounds good. And what would you like to eat?

Yoko: Ummm… I (4.　　　　　　　　) Italian food today.

Anne: OK. Well, Yoko, do you (5.   ) Ken and Greg?

Yoko: Sure. The more, the merrier. But I remember Greg doesn't (6.   ).
Right?

Anne: Yes, that's true. He knows he is tone-deaf. He is (7.   ).

Yoko: But I think it's OK. He can (8.   ) anyway.

▶ **Grammar Part II** More about Infinitives and Gerunds

Focal Point 5: 動名詞< doing ［〜すること］>は、①主語や補語、②動詞の目的語、③前置詞
の目的語になる。

① **主語や補語**

Changing habits is not so easy. ［習慣を変えることは、そんなに簡単なことではありません］

My job is **baking** bread. ［私の仕事はパンを焼くことです］

Seeing is **believing**. ［見ることは信じること（百聞は一見にしかず）］

② **動詞の目的語**

My father doesn't like **playing** video games. ［父はゲームをするのが好きではない］

　　☞ 意味上の主語を表す場合< A（所有格または目的格）+ doing >

　　My father doesn't like **my playing** video games. ［父は私がゲームをするのが好きではない］

　　I'm sure of **him winning** the game. ［彼が試合に勝つことを確信している］

　　☞ 否定形は not doing

　　I'm sure of him **not winning** the game. ［彼が試合に勝てないことを確信している］

③ **前置詞の目的語**

How **about meeting** for lunch tomorrow? ［明日ランチをするのはどうですか］

He left **without saying** goodbye. ［彼はサヨナラも言わずに去った］

Is she interested **in taking** care of a dog? ［彼女は犬の世話に関心があるだろうか］

The building is in danger **of falling down**. ［そのビルは倒壊する危険がある］

You need to concentrate **on studying**. ［勉強に集中する必要があるね］

I'm looking forward **to hearing** from you. ［お返事がいただけるのを楽しみにしています］

Focal Point 6: 不定詞 <to *do*（動詞の原形）> と動名詞 <*doing*> とで意味が異なる動詞

Please remember **to lock** the door when you leave. ［出かけるときは、ドアの鍵を閉めることを覚え
ておいてください］

I clearly remember **locking** the door. ［私はドアを閉めたことをはっきりと覚えています］

She has **forgotten to come** here. ［彼女はここに来るのを忘れてしまった］

I will *never* **forget visiting** this museum. ［この博物館に来たことを決して忘れない］

　*forget -ing は否定文で用いられることが多い。

I **regret to inform** you that you have not been selected. ［残念ながら落選となりました］

I **regret** *not* **choosing** you. ［あなたを選ばなかったことを後悔している］

I **tried to use** this app but it did not work. [このアプリを使おうとしたが、うまくいかなかった]
I **tried using** this app and didn't like it. [このアプリを使ってみたが、気に入らなかった]

動名詞を目的語とする主な動詞	不定詞を目的語とする主な動詞
admit, avoid, consider, deny, enjoy, escape, finish, imagine, mind, miss, practice, quit, suggest, give up, put off	agree, care, decide, desire, expect, hope, manage, mean, need, offer, plan, pretend, promise, refuse, seem, tend (be likely), want, wish
He **admitted cheating** on the test.(=He admitted (that) he had cheated on the test.) Paul **suggested staying** at the hotel. (= Paul **suggested** (that) **we stay** at the hotel.)	Would you **care to join** us for dinner? He **promised to pick** her **up** from the airport.

▶ **Exercise II**

A. Listen to the recording and complete each sentence.   🎧DL 36   ◎ CD 36

1. (   ) time. We have to finish this by five o'clock today.
2. Please don't (   ) the door when you leave.
3. I (   ) a quick phone call.
4. Long time no see! I'm so (   ) again.

B. Correct the error, if any, in each sentence.

1. I suggested to go in my car.
    [私は私の車で行こうと提案しました]

2. I will never forget meeting you.
    [あなたにお会いしたことを決して忘れないでしょう]

3. If you wish to discuss this matter further, please do not hesitate contacting me.
    [もしこの件をさらに議論したければ、遠慮なく私に連絡してください]

C. Put the Japanese sentences into English by filling in the missing information.

1. 私は彼の連絡先の番号を聞かなったことを今後悔しています。

   I now regret (   ) for his contact number.

2. 一人暮らしに慣れました。 [get used to ～]

   I've finally (   ) alone.

3. **A:** もし聞いてもよければ、何歳ですか。 [mind A *doing* ～]

   If you don't (   ), how old are you?

   B: いいですよ。先週 20 歳になったばかりです。

   No problem. I just turned twenty last week.

▶ **Basic Phrases in Social Settings**

A. How did your parents get to know each other? と聞かれた。そういえば、最初のデートで、父が遅刻して母は怒っていたらしい。 On their first date, **she was angry at**_____ _____ _____ _____	B. 昨日は何のパーティーだったの？と聞かれた。友人が Congratulations! と、私の結婚を祝ってくれたことを伝えたい。。 My friends congratulated me _____ _____ _____ _____

▶ Final Touch

A. Choose a suitable expression for each situation. There may be more than one correct answer.

1. 「あなたはそのセミナーにスーツとネクタイを着て行く必要はありません」と、伝える。
   - (A) You're not necessary to wear a suit and tie to the seminar.
   - (B) It's not necessary to wear a suit and tie to the seminar.
   - (C) You don't need to wear a suit and tie to the seminar.

2. 「このような天気で外出したことは、とても愚かだった」と、弟に対して注意する。
   - (A) It was very foolish of you to go out in weather like this.
   - (B) You were very foolish to go out in weather like this.
   - (C) To go out in weather like this was foolish for you.

3. 「すみません、私たちの写真を撮って頂けませんか」と、近くにいる人に依頼する。
   - (A) Excuse me. Would you mind taking a picture of us, please?
   - (B) Excuse me. Would you mind me taking a picture of us, please?
   - (C) Excuse me. Could you please take a picture of us?

▶ Wrap-Up Writing

Answer the questions in English.

Question 1: Where would you like to go and what would you like to do there during winter vacation?

ex. I would like to go to Osaka during winter vacation and visit Universal Studios Japan and Kaiyukan.

Question 2: What kinds of activities do you enjoy the most in your spare time?

ex. I usually enjoy watching American movies or TV shows at home in my spare time. Sometimes, I go cycling with friends if the weather is good.

Question 3: What's your biggest regret in life which you will never forget?

ex. I regret not taking the opportunity to study abroad the most. I should have taken the chance.

Relative Pronouns

Relative Pronouns (1)

Main Points

● 主格の関係代名詞（who, which, that）には、「接続詞」と「代名詞」の働きと先行詞（名詞句）に情報を追加し、限定・明確化する働きがあることを学ぶ。

● 先行詞に合わせて関係代名詞を選ぶことができる。

▶ **Preparation I**

Write or choose a suitable answer for each question.

---

1. What kind of company do you want to work for?

I want to work for a company which . . .

[Vocabulary Box]

give the chance to learn new things / fit my personality / has a clear vision and identity / filled with

passionate people / pay a high salary / offer good fringe benefits

---

2. 留学生がスーパーで目にした食品を説明して欲しいと言っている。

Persimmon

What is persimmon?

a. Persimmon is a fruit which tastes sweet and contains more vitamin C than lemons.

b. Persimmon is a fruit that taste sweet and contain more vitamin C than lemons but tastes sweet.

c. Persimmon is a fruit whose taste sweet and contain more vitamin C than lemons.

▶ Awakening I

A. Greg has a crush on a girl. He is talking about her with Ken. Listen to their conversation and choose the best answer to each question. 🎧 DL 37 ◎ CD 37

1. What is NOT true about the girl?
   a. Her name is Anne.
   b. She wears a dress.
   c. Her boyfriend is Ken.

2. What warning did Ken give Greg?
   a. She already loves someone else.
   b. Greg will break up with her.
   c. Ken will beat Greg up if he breaks her heart.

B. Listen to the conversation again and complete the sentences.

Greg: Hey, Ken. Take a look at the girl over there. She's so cool! Don't you think?

Ken: Which one? I see two girls.

Greg: Oh, I mean the one (1.   ).

Ken: You mean the one (2.   ), right?

Greg: Yes.

Ken: That's Anne. I know her. We went to the same high school. She is nice.

Greg: You know her? Great!

Ken: Greg, listen. She has a boyfriend. She's not available.

Greg: Oh, boy. Thanks for the warning!

▶ Grammar Part I   Subject Relative Pronouns

Focal Point 1: 関係代名詞が「接続詞」と「主語」の役割を果たす。

関係代名詞節

Take a look at the girl **who** is wearing glasses.

- 人が先行詞の場合には who または that を使い、物や動物が先行詞の場合には which または that を使う。ただし、先行詞が人の場合、who を使う方がフォーマルである。
- 関係代名詞に続く動詞の形は、先行詞の人称や数に一致させる。
- 関係詞節は修飾する名詞（句）の直後におかれるため、主節の途中に入ることもある。 ▶ 例文 B

例文		関係詞節			
		関係代名詞	動詞		
A	Take a look at the girl	**who/that**	is wearing	glasses.	
B	The girl	**who/that**	is wearing	glasses	is Anne.
C	This is a four-wheel drive	**which/that**	has	room for eight people.	

that を比較的よく用いる場合	• 先行詞が「限定されるもの」や「その他に選択肢がないもの」のときに which よりも that が好まれる。 • 人が先行詞の場合は、くだけた会話体などでは that も使われる。 • 先行詞が「人 + 人以外」の場合は、that が使われる。

① 特定の 1 つのものであることを表す修飾語（the first, the second, the last, the very, <the + 最上級 >, the same, the only など）を伴う場合

What is the biggest problem that you are facing? [あなたが直面している最も大きな問題は何ですか]

The only thing that matters to me is my family. [私にとって大切な唯一のことは家族です]

    cf. I was the only one who agreed. [私は同意した唯一の人間でした] のように the only があっても who が用いられる場合がある。

The first theater that put on *Wicked* in Japan was in Tokyo.

    [日本で「ウィキッド」を公演した最初の劇場は東京でした]

② 先行詞が「すべて」「まったく〜ない」（all, every, any, no など）を意味する修飾語を伴う場合

They did everything that they could think of to solve the problem.

    [彼らはその問題を解決するのに思いついたことを全て行った]

He talked about all the stories that he knew. [彼は知っている話を全て話してくれた]

③ 疑問詞 who の直後に関係代名詞が続く場合

Who that has read his story can forget it?

    [彼の物語を読んだ人が、それを忘れることができるだろうか]

Focal Point 2: who の所有格は whose であり、<whose + 名詞 > が関係節の主語となる。2 つの文を結ぶ場合、whose は 2 文目にある所有格の代わりとなる。

関係代名詞節

An actor whose baby was born last August was awarded "the Best Father."

▶ Exercise I

A. Listen to the recording and complete each sentence.

DL 38   ◎ CD 38

1. We are looking for someone (   ) Chinese and Japanese.
2. Is there anybody (   )?
3. Please hand the parcel (   ) to Ms. Brown.
4. I'd like to reserve a room (   ).
5. The bus (   ) is bound for London.

B. Choose the most appropriate word or phrase to complete each sentence.

1. The woman (who / that / whose) husband won the Nobel Prize has devoted to supporting him.
2. My friend goes to a university (who / where / that) has a 120-year history.
3. The taxi (that is waiting / which is waiting / what is waiting) in front of the entrance is for you.
4. This is a book (that give / that gives / whose gives) us useful information on how to communicate with others.
5. Say anything (that comes / that come / which come) into your head.

C. Listen to the conversation and choose the best answer to the question.

DL 39   ◎ CD 39

Question: Yoko is asking Anne for a favor. Which report does Yoko need? Choose a, b, c, d, e, or f.

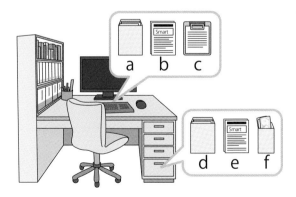

D. Listen to the conversation again and complete the sentences.

Yoko: Anne, could you please bring the report (1.   ) to Room 220 now?

Anne: OK, let's see. Yoko, which report do you need? There are three on your desk.

Yoko: Oh, I'm sorry. I need the one (2.   ). OK?

Anne: Is that the one about "Smart Grammar"?

Yoko: Yes, that's right. The meeting is about to start very soon, so please hurry, Anne.

▶ Basic Phrases in Social Settings

A. もうすぐ父の誕生日。紳士服売り場で買い物。May I help you? とお店の人が声をかけてきた。

お願いします。このスーツに合うネクタイを探しているのですが。

B. 予約したくてお店の人に尋ねると Please take this to the clerk who is standing at the counter. ですって。

短い黒髪の方のことをおっしゃっていますか？

C. ペアになって、A で作成した会話をしてみよう。

▶ Wrap-Up Writing

Referring to the sample definition below, make your own Guess what! and Guess who! questions.

 Sample ▶

Guess what!

It is a thing that usually has four legs but cannot move by itself. Can you guess what it is?

Guess who!

He is a very famous Japanese comedian who speaks a lot at a very fast pace and laughs in a unique manner. His daughter is a fashion model and singer. Can you guess who he is?

Relative Pronouns (2)

Main Points

- 目的格の関係代名詞（who/whom, which, that）は、関係詞節の目的語の働きを持つことを学ぶ。
- 関係代名詞の主格と目的格の違いを学ぶ。

▶ **Preparation II**

Write or choose a suitable expression for each of the given situations.

1. Who is the person you admire most?
   And why?

   The person whom I admire (the) most is…

   because

   _____

   _____

   _____

2. 熱があるので、病院へ行った。You might have the flu. Do you have family or friends who have flu-like symptoms? と聞かれた。

   昨日おしゃべりした友人が、風邪をひいていました。

   a. One of my friends who I talked yesterday had a cold.

   b. One of my friends whom I talked yesterday had a cold.

   c. One of my friends whom I talked with yesterday had a cold.

▶ Awakening II

A. Greg, Yoko, and Anne are talking about a seminar that was held last Monday. Complete the sentences with the correct word or phrases.

🎧 DL 40　◎ CD 40

Greg: I would like to know about the seminar (1.　　　　　　　　　　) last Monday.

Yoko: It was very useful. I learned a lot. You should have joined it.

Greg: I really wanted to⋯ but I had a bad cold last week.

Yoko: Oh, I'm sorry.

Anne: Greg, I have an article (2.　　　　　　　　). This article was written by the speaker of the seminar.

Greg: Thank you, Anne. Could you please photocopy part of it for me?

Anne: Sure thing. Please let me know if there is anything else (3.　　　　　　　　) for you.

▶ Grammar Part II　Object Relative Pronouns

Focal Point 3: 関係代名詞が「接続詞」と「目的語」の役割を果たす。

関係代名詞節

I bumped into the man **who(m)** we met at the party.

- 人が先行詞の場合には that, who, または whom を使い、物や動物が先行詞の場合には that または which を使う。くだけた場面では、that を使うのが一般的。whom は堅い文章体で用いられる場合がある。
- 関係代名詞の後に、主語と動詞が続く。

関係代名詞節

		関係代名詞（目的格）	主語	動詞		
A	The singer	whom/who	I	like	the most	is Taylor Swift.
B	I bumped into the man	whom/who	we	met	at the party.	
C	The company	which	they	visited	last Monday	is in Chiba.

- 目的格の場合、関係代名詞を省略することができる。

関係詞節

＜主語 ＋ 動詞＞

目的格	The movie	(that)	we	saw	last night was very boring.
▶ 比較 主格	The movie		that	was released	last night was very boring.

（主格の場合、関係代名詞の省略はできない）

(×) The movie was released last night was very boring

前置詞 + 関係代名詞の目的格 [whom/which]

The man (whom) she was talking with is the French ambassador.

［彼女が話していた男性がフランスの大使です］

⬇

日常会話であれば、この構文が一般的です。しかし、正式度の高い文書であれば、前置詞 with の後に動詞の is が並ぶのはスタイル上良くないと考えられ、前置詞 with が関係代名詞 whom の前に移動されます。

⬇

The man **with whom** she was talking is the French ambassador.

☞基本的に、前置詞の後には接続詞 that が来ることはありません。

The man with that she was talking is the French ambassador.

I am sorry I cannot give you the source (**which** [**that**]) we got this information **from**.

↔ I am sorry I cannot give you the source **from which** we got this information.

▶ Exercise II

A. Listen to the recording and complete each sentence.　🎧DL 41　◎CD 41

1. The man (　　　　　　　　　　) at the meeting the other day was Mr. Suzuki.
2. Can you contact the people (　　　　　　　　) last Friday?
3. The steak (　　　　　　　　) was expensive but not tender.
4. This is one of the funniest movies (　　　　　　　　).
5. Please jot down all the things (　　　　　　　) during your stay.

B. Choose the most appropriate word or phrase to complete each sentence. Choose φ when a relative pronoun can be omitted.

1. Is that all the work (that, who, whose) you have done today?
2. I have lost the textbook (φ, which, who) is important to read before writing my essay.
3. I have got a problem (φ, who, whose) I would like to talk about with you.
4. The company (which, who, whose) president my brother knows is near here.
5. India is one of the countries (which, who, whose) I want to visit.

C. Put the Japanese sentences into English by filling in the missing information.

1. 私が述べたい点は２つあります。
   There are two points (   ) to make.

2. いまそのタイトルを思い出せないあの映画が、昨晩テレビで放映された。
   The movie (   ) right now was broadcast on TV last night.

3. 私たちはその状況を改善するためにできることは全て試みました。
   We tried everything (   ) to improve the situation.

4. もしあなたが理解できないことがあれば、あなたがしなければならないことは私に聞くことだけです。
   If there is something you don't understand, (   ).

5. A: あなたが入れてくれた珈琲はとてもおいしいです。
   The coffee (   ) is very delicious.
   B: Thank you. I used fresh roasted coffee beans today.

▶ **Final Touch**

A. Choose a suitable expression for each situation. There may be more than one correct answer.

1. 「先週買ったばかりの掃除機が壊れた」と、友人に愚痴る。
   (A) The vacuum cleaner I bought only last week has broken.
   (B) The vacuum cleaner what I bought only last week has broken.
   (C) The vacuum cleaner which I bought only last week has broken.

2. 「ここが、そのブランドを販売している唯一の場所です」と、友人に説明する。
   (A) This is the only place that sells the brand.
   (B) This is the only place which sells the brand.
   (C) This is the only place sells the brand.

3. 「ケンが話していた男性が私たちの新しいコーチだ」と、チームメートに説明する。

    (A)   The man with whom Ken was talking is our new coach.

    (B)   The man whom Ken was talking with is our new coach.

    (C)   The man Ken was talking with is our new coach.

▶ Wrap-Up Writing

Read the article below and circle True (T) or False (F) for each statement.

> When you hear the nickname "The King of Pop," whom do you think of? For many, the person who comes to mind is Michael Jackson. Michael was an American entertainer who made his debut in 1964. Even though he was a young child then, Michael joined "The Jackson 5." It was a group that featured Michael and four of his brothers.
>
> Michael began his career as a solo artist in 1971. Many of the songs which Michael sang became big hits, and one of his original dance moves, called the "moonwalk," started a major dance trend.
>
> Unfortunately, Michael passed away in 2009. The world may never again see another person like Michael Jackson. What he accomplished during his lifetime was amazing!

* make one's debut（デビューする）　feature ~（~を主役にする）　pass away（他界する）　accomplish ~（~を達成する）

1.   T / F   He was an entertainer whose debut was in 1964.
2.   T / F   He was an American who gave a nickname "The King of Pop" to a group of singers.
3.   T / F   He was an artist whose dance moves started a major dance trend.
4.   T / F   Many of the songs which Michael sang became big hits.
5.   T / F   All the members of Michael's family joined "The Jackson 5."

Using the quiz below as a sample, make your own Guess who! quiz question.

Guess who!

This was a man who made his debut in 1964.

He was an American entertainer who was a member of The Jackson 5.

Many of the songs which he sang became big hits.

One of his original dance moves, which was called the "moonwalk," started a major dance trend.

Relative Clauses

Relative Clauses (1)

Main Points

- 名詞（句）を限定・特定させる用法の関係副詞（where, when）を学ぶ。
- 関係副詞・関係代名詞の「非制限用法（継続用法）」を学び、文脈から意味を考える。

▶ Preparation I

Read the situation and answer the questions.

Imagine that you are in the airport in Tokyo. A group of foreign tourists asks you the following questions:

1. Where are some good places to visit in Japan?

2. What can we do there?

3. Combine your answers to the two questions above and make a single sentence.

▶ Awakening I

A. Kathy and Ken are talking about their first date. Listen to their conversation and choose the best answer to each question.　　🎧 DL 42　　◎ CD 42

1. What kind of food does Kathy like?
   a. French
   b. Chinese
   c. Italian

2. Where did they first meet?
   a. at a French restaurant
   b. at a Chinese restaurant
   c. at an Italian restaurant

B. Listen to the conversation again and fill in the blanks.

Kathy: Ken, do you remember the restaurant (1.   )?

Ken: Of course, I do. How could I forget it?

[In Ken's mind]

Uh-oh! There are three possibilities: a French one, a Chinese one, and an Italian one. She likes Italian food, so it must have been the Italian restaurant.

Kathy: From the window by the table (2.   ), we could see roses in the courtyard. They were so beautiful.

Ken: Yeah, yeah, you're right.

[In Ken's mind]

Gosh! She is checking my memory. . . Wait. . . She said courtyard. Only the French restaurant has a courtyard. Thank goodness! It's clear now.

OK, Kathy, let's have lunch at that same French restaurant.

Kathy: I'd love to! Why don't we go there on the anniversary of the day (3.   )?

表現のポイント ▶

Uh-oh! Gosh!「しまった！」「やばい！」

ミスや間違いに気づいたときの驚きを表す感嘆詞です。

Uh-oh, I think I just deleted all my work.［うわあ、やったこと全部消しちゃった気がする］

友達が失敗談をしたときの相づちとしても使えます。

I made a mistake.［やらかしちゃった］—Uh-oh, what happened?［あらら、何したの？］

▶ Grammar Part I Relative Clauses

Focal Point 1: 先行詞が場所を表す場合、関係副詞 where を使う。節には主語と動詞が含まれる。

関係副詞節

I want to visit an area **where** the latest trends in youth culture can be found.

- 先行詞として一般的なものに area, country, city, house, place, room などがある。
- 前置詞 +which の組み合わせは、学術的な文章で where のかわりに用いられる。
  Shibuya is a city **in which** the latest trends in youth culture can be found.

Focal Point 2: 先行詞が時を表す場合、関係副詞 when を使う。節には主語と動詞が含まれる。

関係副詞節

Do you remember the day **when** we moved to this town?

- 先行詞として一般的なものに time, year, season, period, day, moment などがある。
- when を省略することができる。（例）Do you remember the day we moved to this town?
- 前置詞 +which の組み合わせは、フォーマルな用法。
  The majority of people eagerly anticipate the day **on which** they can retire.

制限用法（限定用法）と非制限用法（継続用法）とは・・・
　　関係詞 (who, whose, whom, which, where, when) において、コンマを使わないものを「制限用法（限定用法）」、コンマをつけるものを「非制限用法（継続用法）」という。

関係代名詞の場合
　　< 制限用法 >　　　Greg has two sons **who** are studying economics.
　　　　　　　⇒ Greg has two sons who are studying economics and three sons who are studying business. と言えるように、息子は他にもいる可能性がある。
　　< 非制限用法 >　　Greg has two sons, **who** are studying economics.
　　　　　　　⇒ Greg has two sons, and they are studying economics.
　　　　　　　　［グレッグには息子が 2 人いますが、2 人とも経済学を学んでいます（息子は 2 人だけ）］

関係副詞の場合
　　< 制限用法 >　　　Next month, we are moving to Osaka **where** our grandparents live.
　　　　　　　　　　　［来月、私達は祖父母の住んでいる大阪へ引っ越す］
　　< 非制限用法 >　　Next month, we are moving to Osaka, **where** we will live with our grandparents.
　　　　　　　⇒ Next month, we are moving to Osaka, **and there** we will live with our grandparents.
　　　　　　　　［ 来月、私達は大阪へ引っ越し、そして、そこで祖父母と暮らします]
　　　　　　　　「そして、その場所で…（and there）」を意味する。
　　< 制限用法 >　　　I went to Scotland in May **when** the country has its best weather.
　　　　　　　　　　　［私がスコットランドに行ったのは、そこの気候が最も良い 5 月でした］
　　< 非制限用法 >　　I went to Scotland in May, **when** the weather was like early summer.
　　　　　　　⇒ I went to Scotland in May, **and then** the weather was like early summer.
　　　　　　　　[私がスコットランドに行ったのは 5 月でした。その時の気候は、初夏のようでした]
　　　　　　　　「そして、その時…（and then）」を意味する。
　　☞非制限用法（継続用法）では、that、what、why、how は使われません。

▶ **Exercise I**

A. Listen to the recording and complete each sentence.

🎧 DL 43   ◎ CD 43

1. Let's meet at the hotel (   ).
2. Is this the restaurant (   )?
3. I will never forget the day (   ).
4. Was the day (   ) here July 12?
5. The day has come (   ) to Sendai.

B. Choose the most appropriate word or phrase to complete each sentence.

1. Please tell me the time (which / when / where) you returned here.
2. The office (which / when / where) Ken works is around here.
3. Wednesday is the day (when / , when / on that) I am least busy.
4. **A:** How was the hotel (which / when / where) you stayed in Los Angeles?

   B: The hotel itself was beautiful, but the food served there was a little disappointing.
5. I cannot see him from the place (which / where / in that) I am sitting.

C. Listen to the conversation and choose the best answer to each question.

🎧 DL 44   ◎ CD 44

1. When will Yoko and Anne attend a party?

   (a) on Monday

   (b) on Friday

   (c) on Saturday

   (d) The day is not decided yet.

2. What time will the party start?

   (a) at six

   (b) at seven

   (c) at eight

   (d) The time is not decided yet.

D. Listen to the conversation again and complete the sentences.

Yoko: Anne, will you tell me the day (1.   )? I didn't write it down.

Anne: Well, let's see. My datebook says it's next Friday. And the time (2.   ) is seven.

Yoko: So I should pick you up at your place at six. Is that OK?

Anne: That's great. I can't wait.

▶ Basic Phrases in Social Settings

A. 買い物に誘ったら、I'm sorry I can't hang out with you on Friday. という返事。そうだった、金曜日は観光に行くと言ってた。

それは、あなたが箱根に観光に行く日だね。

B. うわー、すごい！私が実際にグランドキャニオンにいるなんて信じられない。

ここが、私が長い間来たかった場所です。

C. 例を参考にして、誰かの誕生日や誕生年を紹介しましょう。

例 I was born on July 4. That's the day when Americans celebrate their independence.

My grandmother was born in 1939. That's the year when World War II broke out.

▶ Wrap-Up Writing

Referring to the sample definition below, make your own Guess where! and Guess when! questions.

 Sample ▶

Guess where!

It is a place where many people visit to see many kinds of marine creatures. It is in Ikebukuro. Can you guess the place?

Guess when!

It is a national holiday when ceremonies are held for those who have officially become adults. Can you guess the national holiday?

Relative Clauses (2)

Main Points

- 「理由」について情報を追加する関係副詞 why、「方法」「やり方」を説明する the way と how を学ぶ。
- 先行詞を含む関係代名詞 what を学ぶ。

▶ Preparation II

Write or circle a suitable expression for each situation.

---

1. You are late for our date. と、彼女に言われ次のように答えたい。

Please don't be mad. You know it wasn't on purpose. The reason why I'm late is that

_____

_____ .

2. 交通事故を目撃して、その事故が起きた経緯を説明し、最後に友達に以下のように言う。

そのようにして、その事故は起こりました。

a. That's the way it happened.
b. That's the way how it happened.
c. That's how it happened.

▶ Awakening II

A. Ken is talking to Greg. Listen to their conversation and choose the best answer to each question.

🎧DL 45　◎CD 45

1. What did Greg buy?
   a. A pair of jeans that was introduced in a fashion magazine.
   b. A fashion magazine that introduced the jeans Kim usually wears.
   c. A pair of jeans that Kim was talking about.

2. How did Greg feel?
   a. He felt very lucky to sell the item at a good price.
   b. He felt unhappy because the item didn't become cheaper.
   c. He felt happy to buy the item at an unexpectedly cheap price.

B. Listen to the conversation again and complete each sentence.

Ken:　Hey, Greg! Show me (1.　　　　　　　　　) today.

Greg:　You know what? I bought the jeans (2.　　　　　　　　　) the other day.

Ken:　Are they the ones (3.　　　　　　) in the fashion magazine?

Greg:　That's right. I was very lucky. I got a 30 percent discount.

Ken:　Really? Let me take a look at them. ... Oh, cool! I like them. Did you buy the jeans at the store
　　　　(4.　　　　　　　　　)?

Greg:　Yeah, I did.

▶ Grammar Part II　More about Relative Clauses

Focal Point 3: 関係副詞 why は理由を表す。

She told me the reason **why** she went to see him yesterday .
　　［彼女は私に彼女が昨日彼に会いに行った理由を話しました］
There is no reason **why** I have to do it for you .
　　［私があなたのためにそれをしなければならない理由がありません］
The reason I was late this morning is that the car broke down.
　　［今朝私が遅れたのは車が壊れたからです］

・ 上の例文のように、先行詞が the reason の場合、why を使わないで表現することもできる。
・ また、why の代わりに that が使われることもある。
　　This / That is why ＋主語＋動詞…で、「こういうわけで／そういうわけで…」という意味を表す。
　　It's raining. This is why I won't go out. ［雨が降っています。こういうわけで出かけたくありません］

Focal Point 4: the way と how は「方法」を表す。the way how のように共に使われることはない。

構造上のパターン：the way (in which, that) ＋主語＋動詞・・・

構造上のパターン：how ＋主語＋動詞・・・

I do not like **the way** she speaks . [私は彼女の話し方が好きではありません]

That is **the way** we do it here . [それは私たちがここでそれをする方法です]

He demonstrated **how** the machine works .

　[彼はその機械がどのように動くかを実際にやってみせてくれた]

Can you explain **how** it happened ? [それがどのようにして起こったのかを説明できますか]

・　the way と how は共に用いられない。
・　This/That is how＋主語＋動詞…で、「このようにして／そのようにして…」という意味を表す。
　　This is how this accident happened. [このようにしてこの事故は起こりました]

Focal Point 5: 関係代名詞 what は「〜すること（もの）」を表す。先行詞なしで用いる。
　　　　　　　　what から成る名詞節は、主語、目的語、補語となる。具体的にそれが何である
　　　　　　　　かを示さず、漠然と「こと・もの」として示し、それによって相手の注意を引き
　　　　　　　　付ける。

① 主語として

　What I am saying applies to all of you. [私が言っていることは皆さん全員に当てはまります]
② 動詞の目的語として

　Tell me **what** you think about my plan . [私の計画についてあなたが思うところを教えてください]
③ 前置詞の目的語として

　Please pay attention to **what** I am going to say . [私がこれから言うことに注意を払ってください]
④ 補語として

　That is **what** I want . [それが、私が欲しいものです]

▶ **Exercise II**

A. Listen to the recording and complete each sentence.　🎧DL 46　◎CD 46

1. Please tell me the reason (　　　　　　　　　　　　　) yesterday.
2. I don't like the way (　　　　　　　　　).
3. Could you repeat (　　　　　　　　　)?
4. (　　　　　　　　) we moved to a suburb of Tokyo.
5. (　　　　　　　　) they got to know each other better.

B. Ken and Yoko have been sharing an apartment. They have experienced some frustrations as well as enjoyment. Complete each sentence with appropriate words.

Ken: Do you remember the day (1.　　　　　　　　　　) ［私たちが初めて話した日］ to each other?

Yoko: Yes, I can clearly remember (2.　　　　　　　　　) ［私たちが話したこと］ about even now. I miss those days (3.　　　　　　　　　) ［私たちが話すことができた］ about anything together.

Ken: (4.　　　　　　　　　　) ［私たちが今必要としているもの］ is a frank exchange of opinions.

Yoko: I couldn't agree more. . . and may I say something?

C. Put the Japanese sentences into English by filling in the missing information.

1. 私が生まれ育った街は国分寺です。

   The city (　　　　　　　　　　　) and grew up is Kokubunji.

2. 私がこの会社で働きたい理由がいくつかあります。

   There are several reasons (　　　　　　　　　　　　　) for this company.

3. 私はへとへとです。私が今必要なものは十分な睡眠です。

   I'm worn out. (　　　　　　　　　　　) now is a good sleep.

4. **A:** Loop 7 is congested with traffic for about three kilometers.

   B: そういうわけで、バスが予定より大幅に遅れているのです。

   (　　　　　　　　　　　) the bus is for behind schedule.

5. **A:** How do you feel now? Are you OK?

   B: 私が今どのように感じているのかを言葉にするのは難しいです。

   It is difficult to put (　　　　　　　　　　　) now into words.

▶ **Final Touch**

A. Choose a suitable expression for each situation. There may be more than one correct answer.

1. 「そのようにして、その問題を解決しました」と、友人に説明する。
   (A) That's the way how we solved the problem.
   (B) That's the way which we solved the problem.
   (C) That's how we solved the problem.

2. 「ここが、ケンの父親が経営しているお店だ」と、友人に言う。
   (A) This is the store where Ken's father runs.
   (B) This is the store that Ken's father runs.
   (C) This is the store Ken's father runs.

3. 「ケンの兄のタロウは、そのスーパーで働いていますが、私の友達です」と、友人に説明する。

    (A)   Ken's brother Taro who works at the supermarket is a friend of mine.

    (B)   Ken's brother Taro, who works at the supermarket, is a friend of mine.

    (C)   Ken's brother Taro, that works at the supermarket, is a friend of mine.

▶ Wrap-Up Writing

A. Read the passage while paying attention to *where*, *when*, *why*, and *what*. Then answer the questions.

    Kyoto is a place where many people want to go. Throughout the city, there are countless temples, shrines, and other priceless historical structures. And if you want to enjoy a real Japanese festival, you should visit in July. July is the month when ***Gion Matsuri***, the festival of Yasaka Shrine, takes place. It is the most famous festival in Japan.

There are some other reasons why so many people would like to visit Kyoto. Kyoto offers a rich culinary tradition. Its local food culture is diverse and ranges from aristocratic ***kaiseki ryori*** course dinners to the vegetarian ***shojin ryori*** of monks. Besides the delicious food, you can enjoy beautiful cherry blossoms in April and colorful autumn leaves in November in Kyoto. What one experiences in Kyoto makes life rich and beautiful! You must go!

---

* culinary tradition（食の伝統）vegetarian（菜食主義の）monk（修道僧）

1)   What is the best month to enjoy a real Japanese festival in Kyoto?

2)   What are some of the reasons why people want to visit Kyoto?

3)   What makes life rich and beautiful, according to the author of the passage?

B. Write a passage about a place that you recommend visiting using where, when, why, what, etc. Use the passage above and sample below to help you.

    Sample ▶

Good afternoon, everyone. Let me tell you about (the name of the place) today.

There are several reasons why I recommend you to visit there.

_____ is a place where _____ .

_____ is the month when _____ .

Unit 12 Comparatives and Superlatives

比較・最上級

Comparing Things (1)

Main Points

● 何かを比較して、「優劣」、「大小」、「強弱」などにおける差［違い］を述べる表現を学ぶ。

▶ **Preparation I**

Write or choose a suitable expression for each situation.

---

1. Who is faster, Yuto or Hayate?

Name	50 meters
Yuto	6.5 seconds
Hayate	6.3 seconds

According to the results, Hayate is

_____ than Yuto.

---

2. お兄さんは何歳年上と聞かれて。

私より 2 歳年上なの。

a. He is older than me for two years.
b. He is two years older than me.
c. He is two years as old as me.

▶ **Awakening I**

A. Anne and Greg are at a computer shop. They are taking a look at laptop computers. Listen to the conversation and choose the best answer to each question.

🎧 DL 47　◎ CD 47

1. What is Anne's budget?
   a. It's 76,000 yen.
   b. It's up to 70,000 yen.
   c. It's 68,000 yen.

110

2. What is Anne likely to do next?

    a. She is likely to go to a bank to get money.

    b. She is likely to buy a discounted computer.

    c. She is likely to think twice before buying.

B. Listen to the conversation again and complete the sentences.

Anne: It's (1.   ) than my budget. I can't afford to buy a computer that costs (2.   ) 70,000 yen.

Greg: All right. Then, how about this one? It's on sale – 20% off! Its price is 8,000 yen (3.   ). And its specs are (4.   ).

Anne: Good. It is within my budget. [*Picking up the computer*] This is a little heavy to carry, but that's OK. I don't often carry my computer anyway. I will take this one.

▶ **Grammar Part I**　Comparing Two Things

Focal Point 1: A + be 動詞 + <形容詞・副詞の比較級> + than + B で表す。
規則変化（-er 型、more/less 型）と不規則変化（例：good-better）がある。

Ai is **taller than** Yoko (is).

Getting out of bed in summer is **less difficult than** in winter.

Tomoko can speak French **better than** English.

My sister has **more books than** me < または than I (do)>.
　☞差の大小を表す表現や具体的な差（数値）は比較級の前に加える。

George is now <u>eight centimeters</u> **taller than** he was a year ago.

The number of visitors was <u>much</u> **lower than** expected.

Your room is <u>far</u> **larger than** mine.

Focal Point 2: 何と何を比べているかを明確にする。

The sun rises earlier <u>in summer</u> than <u>in winter</u>. ［太陽は冬よりも夏のほうが早く昇る］
　☞ in summer と in winter を比較しているので、2つ目の in は省略できない。
<u>The population of Japan</u> is far less than <u>that of China</u>.
　　［日本の人口は中国（の人口）よりもずっと少ない］
　☞ the population of Japan と the population of China を比較しているので、that (= the population) of は省略できない。

Focal Point 3: AとBを比べた結果、そこに差［違い］が（ほぼ）ない場合に使われる。

A +be 動詞 + as 形容詞・副詞の原級 as + B →（AはBと同じぐらい〜だ）

Ai is 20 years old, and Yoko is also 20. ［アイは20歳で、ヨウコも20歳です］
アイの年齢とヨウコの年齢を比べると…
　⇒ Ai is as old as Yoko (is). ［アイはヨウコと同じ年です］

Mr. Okada speaks English **as well as** Ms. Hayashi (does).
　［岡田さんは、林さんと同じくらい上手に英語を話します］

☞ not as [so] 〜 as. . . :「…ほど〜ない」
　Our presentation wasn't as [so] good as theirs. ［私たちのプレゼンは彼らのほどよくありませんでした］
☞ as 形容詞・副詞の原級 as possible ／ as 形容詞・副詞の原級 as one can :「できるだけ〜」
　I ran to the station as fast as I could [as fast as possible] to catch the last train.
　　［終電に間に合うようにできるだけ速く走りました］

▶ Exercise I

A. Listen to the recording and complete each sentence.　　🎧 DL 48　◎ CD 48

1. This red backpack is (　　　　　　　　　　　　　) the black one.
2. The price of this blue backpack is (　　　　　　　　　　　　) that of the red one.
3. This red backpack is (　　　　　　　　) the green one.
4. Yoko can sing (　　　　　　) you. She's a very good singer.
5. Please send us your resume (　　　　　　　).

B. Match the sentences.

1. This box is too small to hold everything. 　　　[　　]
2. You're talking too fast. 　　　[　　]
3. I think you should go and see the client. 　　　[　　]
4. Minami isn't as old as Greg. 　　　[　　]
5. The weather here is very cold. 　　　[　　]

　a. You know him better than I do.
　b. Could you speak more slowly?
　c. I need a much bigger box.
　d. I want to move somewhere warmer.
　e. She is two years younger than him.

C. Put the Japanese into English to complete each conversation.

1. A: Shall we go there by car or by train?

   B: Let's drive. It's (   ) and (   ).

   車で行こうよ。車で行く方がより便利だし、かなり安いよ。

2. A: Yoko, can you walk (   )? We're going to be late.

   ヨウコ、もう少し速く歩けない？遅刻しちゃうよ。

   B: No, I can't walk any (   ) than I'm walking now. Let's take a taxi.

   無理、これ以上に速く歩くことはできません。タクシーに乗りましょう。

3. A: How do you feel now? Do you (   )?

   今の気分はどうですか。気分は良くなりましたか。

   B: No, I still feel bad. Actually, I feel (   ) than this morning.

   いいえ、まだ気分は悪いです。実際、今朝よりも悪くなっています。

   A: Really? You should see a doctor (   ).

   本当ですか。できるだけ早くお医者様に見てもらった方がいいですよ。

▶ Basic Phrases in Social Settings

A. 夏と冬とではどちらが好きですか、
　　と聞かれて。

あなた自身の言葉で…

B. 都会に住むのと田舎に住むのとでは、
　　どちらが好きですか、と聞かれて。

あなた自身の言葉で…

C. ペアになって、AまたはBで作成した会話をしてみよう。

▶ Wrap-Up Writing

You are talking with your friend about which apartment you should rent. Using the dialogue below as a sample, write two reasons why you recommend one over the other.

	Rent	Location	Year Built	Style	Security Deposit
Sakura Apartments	48,000 yen/m	10-min walk to ABC station	1985	Japanese	1 month rent
Urban Mansion	55,000 yen/m	5-min walk to ABC station	2015	Western	1.5 month rent

Sakura Apartments

Urban Mansion

You: What do you think, Greg? I have to call the real estate agent by tomorrow. They're holding the two apartments for me.

Greg: Well, if I were you, I would rent the one in Sakura Apartments. It is old, but **much cheaper**.

You: Yes, you're right. But Urban Mansion is **closer** to the station. It's only 5 minutes away.

Greg: You have a bike, right? So, five minutes is not a big difference.

You: Yeah, that's right, but that apartment has two closets.

Greg: I have an idea. If you work at the izakaya **three hours longer** a week, it will cover the difference.

Comparing Things (2)

Main Points

- 3つ以上のうちで、最も程度が高いことを述べるときに使われる最上級を用いた表現を学ぶ。
- 「～の2倍」、「～の2分の1」ということを述べるときに使われる倍数比較構文を学ぶ。

▶ Preparation II

Write or choose a suitable expression for each situation.

1. Which of the following three sports do you think is the most popular in the world?

   I think _____ .

2. Describe the difference in the prices. Choose the correct one(s).

	Airs	LightFly
Haneda → New Chitose	25,000 yen	12,500 yen

   a. The price of Airs is twice as much as that of LightFly.

   b. The price of Airs is less expensive than that of LightFly.

   c. The price of LightFly is half as much as that of Airs.

▶ Awakening II

A. After several interviews, two people are talking about who should be hired as a part-time server. Listen to their conversation and fill in each blank.

🎧 DL 49   ◎ CD 49

	Gender	Fluency of Japanese	Mother Language(s)	The Length of Stay in Japan (from now)	The Length of Work Experience in the Service Industry (total years)
Candidate A	1)	low intermediate	2)	3)	5)
Candidate B	male	low intermediate	English	4)	6)
Candidate C	male	high intermediate	English	2	2

Memo:

▶ Grammar Part II Comparing Two Things, and Three or More Things

Focal Point 4: as … as の前に分数・倍数をおき「〜の X 倍」「〜の X 分の Y」を表す。

Your room is <u>twice</u> **as large as** mine. ［あなたの部屋は私の 2 倍の広さだ］

This PC's processing speed is <u>five times</u> **as fast as** the old model's.
　　［このパソコンは旧モデルより 5 倍処理が速い］

The population of the town today is <u>half</u> **as large as** that of 30 years ago.
　　［現在の町の人口は 30 年前の半分だ］

The second volume of this novel is <u>two-thirds</u> **as long as** the first.
　　［この小説の第 2 巻は第 1 巻の 3 分の 2 の長さだ］
　　☞ ＜ as ＋数量を表す形容詞＋名詞＋ as ＞

My mother has read <u>three times</u> **as many books as** me ＜または I (have)＞. ［母は私の 3 倍も本を読んでいる］

My brother earns <u>half</u> **as much money as** my father. ［兄の収入は父の半分だ］

Focal Point 5: 「～すればするほど、それだけ・・・」を表す。

The + 比較級 ～ , the + 比較級・・・:「～すればするほど、それだけ・・・」

The more you use your brain, **the smarter** you will become.

［頭を使えば使うほど、あなたは賢くなります］

A: How many people shall we invite to the party? ［パーティーに何人招待しましょうか］

B: **The more**, **the merrier**. ［多ければ多いほど楽しいですよ］

Focal Point 6: 3 つ以上のもの・人のうちで、最も程度が高いことを表す。

『［場所］の中で ／ ［数］のうちで…が最も～です』と表す場合・・・

形容詞の場合

A + be 動詞 + **形容詞の最上級** + **in** ［場所］ ／ **of** ［数］ → （A が ［場所］ の中で／ ［数］ のうちで最も～です）

Greg made the **best** presentation **of** the three. ［3 人のうちで、グレッグが一番良い発表をしました］

She's one of the **quickest** players **on** the team. ［彼女はそのチームの中で最も俊敏な選手の一人です］

It is the **most interesting** movie I have ever seen. ［それは、私が今までに見た映画の中で最も面白いです］

副詞の場合

A + 動詞 + **副詞の最上級** + **in** ［場所］ ／ **of** ［数］ → （A が ［場所］ の中で／ ［数］ のうちで最も～します）

Yoko can type (the) **fastest of** all. ［ヨウコは全員のうちで一番速くタイプができます］

Who left the office (the) **last** yesterday? ［昨日、最後に事務所を出たのは誰ですか］

☞ 副詞の場合は、the を省くことができます。

▶ Exercise II

A. Listen to the recording and complete each sentence.

🎧 DL 50　◉ CD 50

1. The monthly salary of this company is 1.2 times (　　　　　　　　) that of the other company.

2. The buses run (　　　　　　　) on weekends.

3. (　　　　　　　) you get to know him, (　　　　　　　) you will like him.

4. This hotel is (　　　　　　　) in this town.

5. This is (　　　　　　　) I've ever seen.

B. Correct the errors, if any, in the sentences below.

1. Having you here does make things very easier for me.

2. This is one of the most commonly used method.

3. Mr. Lee behaves the most politely in the three men.

4. This is a most unproductive meeting I have ever attended.

5. We probably need to get more two boxes.

C. Put the Japanese sentences into English by filling in the missing information.

1. 最寄りの地下鉄の駅へ行く道を教えていただけませんか。

   Could you tell me the way to (   ) subway station?

2. A: 3つのプロジェクトのうちでどれが一番費用対効果が高いですか。

   (   ) cost effective (   ) the three projects?

   B: It is Project C.

3. 私たちはできるだけ短時間でこれを終わらせる必要があります。 [quickly]

   We need to get this finished (   ).

4. それを仕上げるのには私たちが思っていたよりずっと時間がかかりました。

   It took (   ) we had expected to complete it.

5. A: コーヒーと紅茶ではどちらが好きですか。

   Which (   ), coffee or tea?

   B: コーヒーの方が好きです。

   I like coffee (   ).

   A: では、ブラック、ミルク入り、エスプレッソ、カフェインレスではどれが一番好きですか。

   (   ), then, black coffee, coffee with milk, espresso, or decaf coffee?

   B: ブラックが一番好きです。

   I like black coffee (   ).

▶ **Final Touch**

A. Choose a suitable expression for each situation. There may be more than one correct answer.

1. 「日本の人口はこの国の約3倍です」と説明する。

   (A) The population of Japan is about three times of this country.

   (B) The population of Japan is about three times as large as that of this country.

   (C) The population of Japan is about three times as large as this country.

2. 「これからもっと気をつけます」と仕事場の店長に言う。

   (A) From now on, I will be more careful.

   (B) From now on, I will be very careful.

   (C) From now on, I will be much careful.

3. 「私の新しいコンピュータは、前のものよりもずっと速くて、軽いです」と説明する。

   (A) My new computer is much faster and lighter than my old one was.

   (B) My new computer is a lot faster and more light than my old one was.

   (C) My new computer is much faster and very lighter than my old one was.

▶ Wrap-Up Writing

Put the Japanese into English. Then make your own sentences.

	Bike A	Bike B	Bike C
Price	20,000 yen	21,000 yen	40,000 yen
Weight	18 kg	14 kg	9 kg
Speed	25 km/h	20 km/h	50 km/h

1) Bike A は Bike B とほぼ同じ値段です。 [expensive]

   Bike A is _____ .

2) Bike C は Bike A の 2 倍の値段で、3 つの中で一番高いです。

   Bike C is _____ .

3) Bike C の価格は私の予算より少し高いですですが、速くてかっこいいので買おうと思います。

                                         [high, budget]

   The price of Bike C is _____ , but I'm going to buy it because

   it's fast and cool.

Your own sentences:

Bike A _____ .

Bike B _____ .

Bike C _____ .

Conjunctions (1)

Main Points

● 「時」を表す when、「理由・原因」を表す because、「条件」を表す if などの接続詞を学ぶ。
● 状況に合わせて接続詞を使い分けることができる。

▶ **Preparation I**

Write or choose a suitable expression for each situation.

---

1. Why did you choose to study at university?

I chose to study at university

_____

_____

_____ .

---

2. 母親が、包帯の巻かれた手を見て驚いている。状況を説明しよう。

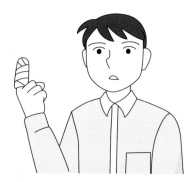

料理をしている最中に、ナイフで
指を切った

a. While I was cooking, I cut my finger with a knife.

b. As I was cooking, I cut my finger with a knife.

c. Once I was cooking, I cut my finger with a knife.

▶ Awakening I

A. Greg is writing a report, and Ken is waiting for Greg. Listen to the recording and select the best answer to each question.   🎧 DL 51   ◎ CD 51

1. What is true about Greg?
   a. He has two more reports to finish.
   b. He finished writing the report 30 minutes ago.
   c. He will finish writing before the party starts.

2. What is true about Ken?
   a. He is willing to help Greg with his report.
   b. He will cancel the party.
   c. He has an article to read.

B. Listen to the recording again and complete the sentences with the correct conjunctions.

Ken will wait (   ) Greg has finished writing the report.

Greg guesses he can finish the report about 30 minutes (   ) the party starts.

(   ) he is waiting, Ken will take a look at the article he has to read.

▶ Grammar Part I   Conjunctions

従属節	・「節（clause）」には、主語と動詞が含まれる。 ・主節が文の骨格となり、それだけで文として意味が成り立つ。一方、従属節は等位接続詞（and, or, but）以外の接続詞や関係代名詞に続く節を指し、それだけでは文が成り立たない。

Focal Point 1: 従属節は、主節の①前に置かれる場合、②後ろに置かれる場合、そして③中間に置かれる場合がある。

① 先に状況を説明してから本題（主節の内容）に入る場合、通例コンマが副詞節の後に置かれる。

When I was a child, I loved Godzilla movies.［子供のとき、私はゴジラ映画が大好きでした］

Although the sun was shinning, it was quite cold.［太陽が輝いていましたが、かなり寒かったです］

② 本題（主節の内容）を述べ、情報を追加的に加える場合。コンマは通例付けない。ただし、逆接を表す副詞節の場合、通例コンマが使われる。

You should insure your house **in case** there is a fire.［火事に備えて、家に保険をかけるべきです］

I thought he was right, **although** I didn't say so at the time.
　　［私は彼が正しいと思いましたが、その時はそう言いませんでした］

③ 主語を示して、それに関連する事項を急いで付け加える場合。通例、副詞節の前後にコンマが置かれる（会話では用いられない）。

Honey, **since** it is natural, is good for your health.［ハチミツは自然のものなので健康に良いです］

「時」を示す接続詞	「原因・理由」を示す接続詞	「条件」を表す接続詞
when「～するときに（順序を表す）」、as「～しながら（同時性を表す）」 while「～している間（ずっと）」 as soon as「～するとすぐに」 before「～する前に」 until/till「～するまで」 since「～して以来」 after「～した後に」 once「いったん～すれば」 every time「毎回～するごとに」 by the time「～するまでには（すでに）」	because (1) 相手にとって新しい情報 (2) 主節の内容の正当性を主張 (3) 文尾に置かれることが多い since/as：相手にも既知の情報、主節の内容ほど重要性がない now (that)「～となった今は、今や～だから」	if「もし～なら（相手に条件を提示）」 unless「もし～ということがないなら、～でない限り」 only if「～する場合に限り」 even if「たとえ～しても」 in case「～する場合に備えて、～するといけないから」

▶ **Exercise I**

A. Choose the correct conjunction to complete the sentence.

1. (When, Until, By the time) I am tired, I tend to make mistakes.

2. You should always exercise (even if, only if, unless) it's only 10 minutes a day.

3. We are all set. (While, Unless, Since) something unexpected happens, I'll come and see you at 9:00 a.m. tomorrow.

4. She looks bad-tempered, but she is kind at heart. You'll like her (till, while, once) you get to know her.

5. (Now that, If, In case) my parents have gone on vacation, let's have a party.

B. Match the parts to make appropriate sentences.

1. Tim is working hard   a. because she is not satisfied with her present job.

2. Kathy is looking for a better job   b. before she attends her friend's wedding.

3. My sister wants to buy a new dress   c. when she was younger.

4. Susan used to buy new clothes every month   d. even if the other members agree.

5. Mr. Johnson will not accept this proposal   e. because he has got an exam next week.

C. Complete each sentence with an appropriate conjunction.

1. The phone rang just (   ) I was leaving.

2. You should come home (   ) it gets dark.

3. (   ) you were not in class yesterday, we made the decision without you.

4. I will come and see you after the meeting, (   ) time permits.

5. We'll be able to achieve our targets (   ) if each one of us works closely together.

▶ Basic Phrases in Social Settings

A. チューターとして相談窓口で対応中。
学生証を失くしてしまったという留
学生がやってきた。

学生証を紛失した時は、警察にも届けを
しっかりしてください。
Please be sure to alert the police

_____ .

B. 定期試験なのに電車が遅延。学務課に
行って状況を説明しないと。

電車が遅延して、試験に遅刻しました。

▶ Wrap-Up Writing

A. Ken and Anne are talking about their plans for their winter vacations. Listen to the conversation and choose the best answer to each question.   DL 52   ◎ CD 52

1. Why does Anne give up on her hope to go back to America during winter break?
    a. Because plane tickets will cost too much.
    b. Because she needs to work at a store.
    c. Because she is going to go skiing.

2. What will Anne most likely do next?
    a. She will cancel her trip to America.
    b. She will check her shifts at her part-time job.
    c. She will call her friends to confirm their ski plan.

B. What do you think Anne should do if her work schedule conflicts with the ski plan? Write your opinion, and then exchange your idea(s) with your partner. Try to use conjunctions when possible.

Conjunctions (2)

Main Points

- 「逆接」を表す although、「対比・対照」を表す while、「程度」を表す so (such) … that などを理解する。
- 接続詞を使い、状況を適切に描写することができる。

▶ Preparation II

Write or choose a suitable expression for each situation.

1. What is specifically different about your life now compared with your life before you entered university?

              .

2. Do you remember the surprise party?
   と聞かれて。

ずいぶん前のことになりますが、そのパーティーは今でも記憶に残っています

I can still remember the party,

  a. however it was so long ago.

  b. even though it was so long ago.

  c. despite it was so long ago.

▶ Awakening II

A. **Greg is talking about his summer vacation. Listen to his speech and choose appropriate answers to the questions. There may be more than one correct answer.**

DL 53　◎ CD 53

1. What is Greg's plan?

   a. He will spend the vacation with Yoko's family.

   b. He will join a volunteer organization.

   c. He will assist a person who designs new houses.

2. What is true about Greg's speech?

   a. He is inviting more people to participate.

   b. Some students might think his plan is unusual.

   c. He must cancel his plan if it rains.

B. **Complete the sentences from the speech. Then think about the meaning of the phrase you wrote. Which of the following functions does the phrase have: (a) to contrast, (b) to give two options or alternatives, (c) to state a purpose, or (d) to give a reason?**

1. (　　　　　) it may seem unusual to some of you, our plan is to volunteer with an organization that builds homes for families in need.

[　]

2. (　　　　　) we like to think about it or not, many people are in difficult situations due to earthquakes, sickness, or even bad luck.

[　]

3. Volunteering over summer vacation sounded like (　　) a great opportunity (　　) I jumped at the chance.

[　]

4. Keep your fingers crossed for good weather (　　　　)(　　　　) we will be able to help many families!

[　]

▶ **Grammar Part II** More about Conjunctions

Focal Point: 前置詞句との違いに気を付ける。節には**主語**と**動詞**が含まれる。
読むとき・聞くときに接続詞に注意を向けると、話の流れを理解しやすくなる。

「逆接」、「期待に沿わない状況」を示す	「対比・対照」を表す副詞節を導く	「程度」を示す
although と though：文頭では「〜ではあるけれども」という意味、文尾では「もっとも〜だけれども」という意味を持つ even though：強意語 even で though を修飾しており、「たとえ〜でも、たとえ〜だとしても」という意味を持つ	while：「〜なのに対して、一方では〜」という意味を持つ whereas：「〜であるのに対して [反して]、〜である一方で」という意味を持つ while：「（逆接的に）〜だけれども」という意味もある	so. . . that：「とても…なので〜」という意味を表す。…の部分に、形容詞または副詞が入る such. . . that：「とても…なので〜」という意味を表す。…の部分に、形容詞＋名詞が入る
「目的」、「結果」を示す	**「様態・状態」を表す副詞節を導く**	**Whether 〜 or not の用法**
so that：[目的]「〜するために、〜となるように」という意味を持つ so that:[結果]「それで、そのため」という意味を持つ	as：「〜のように」という意味や、「〜のままで」という意味を持つ	whether 〜 or not / whether or not 〜：「〜であろうと（なかろうと）」という意味を持つ

	接続詞	前置詞句
理由（原因）	because	because of, due to, owing to「〜のために」 Due to the rain, the tennis match was stopped for about 20 minutes.
逆接	although	in spite of, despite「〜にもかかわらず、〜をよそに」 The event was held in spite of bad weather.
期間	while	during「（特定の期間の）〜の間はずっと，〜の間に」 You are not allowed to use your smartphone during the exam.

☞ due to 〜と owing to 〜の方が because of 〜よりも堅い表現，despite 〜の方が in spite of 〜よりも堅い表現だと言われる。
☞ 前置詞（during など）や群前置詞（because of など）の後には、名詞（句）が続く。

▶ **Exercise II**

A. Listen to the recording and complete each sentence.

🎧 DL 54   ◎ CD 54

1. She arrived early, (   ).

2. (   ), this is the reality.

3. I was (   ) I fell asleep at my desk.

4. We wasted three hours waiting in the rain (   )!

5. Today was a class observation day. My father came to school, (   ).

B. Complete each sentence with the correct words.

1. **Yoko:** Did you have the BBQ last weekend?

   Anne: No, we couldn't (   ) (   ) a sudden downpour. It was postponed until next
   Saturday.

2. **Greg:** Do you have something to eat, Mom?

   Mom: I think there is some frozen pizza in the fridge. But. . . it's not that time yet.

   Greg: I feel hungry (   ) (   ) I had a big lunch.

C. Choose the correct conjunction or words to complete the sentence.

1. _____ you might know, Yoko is leaving Japan in one week.
   (A) As   (B) Because   (C) Since   (D) Due to

2. I fell asleep while I _____ a movie.
   (A) watch   (B) am watching   (C) watched   (D) was watching

3. _____ Christmas comes, I want to find a girlfriend.
   (A) Until   (B) By the time   (C) Though   (D) While

4. The old system was fairly complicated, _____ the new system is really very simple.
   (A) as   (B) because of   (C) whereas   (D) now that

▶ Basic Phrases in Social Settings

A. 台風が近づいている日の１限。スマホで確認したら「終日休講」だって…連絡が遅いよね。教室にいるクラスメイトに伝えよう。

今日は台風のため、終日休講だって。

B. 白熱した議論があった授業の後、クラスメイトに Why didn't you say anything during the discussion? と言われた。

とても混乱していたので考えをまとめることができなかったんだよ。

▶ Final Touch

A. Choose a suitable expression for each situation. There may be more than one correct answer.

1. 「その小包を受け取ったらすぐに、電話します」と友人に言う。
   a. Right after I receive the package, I'll call you.
   b. As soon as I receive the package, I'll call you.
   c. When I receive the package, I'll call you.

2. 「グァム滞在中に、一度アンに会っただけです」と言う。
   a. I only saw Anne once during staying in Guam.
   b. I only saw Anne once during my stay in Guam.
   c. I only saw Anne once while I was staying in Guam.

3. 「私たちのチームは負けましたが、いい試合でした」と言う。
   a. Though our team lost, it was a good game.
   b. However our team lost, it was a good game.
   c. Although our team lost, it was a good game.

▶ Wrap-Up Writing

Which do you prefer, traveling abroad or traveling around Japan?

Compare your answer with your classmate's and summarize your opinions. Try to use conjunctions when possible.

Sample ▶

Natsuki loves to travel abroad, whereas I prefer to travel around Japan. Both of us agree that the cost of outbound tours is equal to or sometimes even cheaper than domestic tours.

_____

_____

_____

_____

_____

Conditionals

Conditionals (1)

Main Points

● 時制を変えることにより、仮想の世界を表すことができることを学ぶ。

● 現在の事実に反する仮定法過去「もし〜なら、…だろうに」を学ぶ。

● 過去の事実に反する仮定法過去完了「もし〜だったなら、…だったろうに」を学ぶ。

▶ Preparation I

Write or choose a suitable expression for each situation.

1. Where would you like to go if you had a lot of money?

If I had a lot of money, I _____

_____

_____

2. 運転免許学科試験の勉強を手伝って くれた友達に合格の報告をする。

君の助けがなかったら、
試験に合格していなかったよ

a. If it were not for your help, I couldn't pass the test.

b. If it had not been for your help, I couldn't have passed the test.

c. If it had not been for your help, I couldn't pass the test.

▶ **Awakening I**

A. Anne and Ken are talking about their plans for their spring vacations. Listen to the conversation and choose the best answer to each question. 🎧 DL 55　◎ CD 55

1. Which country does Ken want to visit?
   a. Spain
   b. Brazil
   c. Not mentioned

2. Why does Anne give up on her plans for traveling?
   a. Because her efforts to pass the test came to nothing.
   b. Because the Rio Carnival will begin in March.
   c. Because she has no money to spare.

B. Listen to the conversation again and complete the sentences.

Anne:　Ken, where (1.　　　　　　　　　　) you like to go during our spring break if you
　　　　(2.　　　　　　　　　　)?

Ken:　. . . If I (3.　　　　　　　　　), well, let's see. . . I (4.　　　　　　　　　　)
　　　　to go to Spain and visit La Sagrada Familia in Barcelona. How about you, Anne?

Anne:　Me? I wish I (5.　　　　　　　　　) to Brazil and watch the Rio Carnival. But, in
　　　　reality, money is tight right now, so I can't afford to travel.

Ken:　I know what you mean. Me, neither.

▶ **Grammar Part I** Conditionals

Focal Point 1: 仮定法過去：現在の事実に反することを仮定・想像・願望するため、過去形を使う。

基本形　If + 主語 + 動詞（過去形）〜 , 主語 + **would/could/might** + 動詞の原形 ･･･.
　　　　（* be 動詞は主語にかかわらず were を用いるのが一般的）

現実：　It is not fine today, so we can't see Mt. Fuji from here.
　　　　［今日は晴れていない。だから、ここから富士山は見えない］

仮定：　If it **were** fine today, we **could see** Mt. Fuji from here.
　　　　［もし今日晴れていれば、ここから富士山が見えるのに］

・仮定法過去を利用した定型表現

もし私があなただったら…

If I were you (If I were in your position), I wouldn't worry about it.［もし私があなただったら、それについて心配しないだろう］

もし・・・がなかったら

If it were not for weekends, I would go insane.［もしも週末がなかったら、気が変になりそうだよ］

If it were not for your help, I couldn't do the work.［もし君の助けがなかったら、仕事にならないだろう］

・if がないパターン（主語・動詞の倒置）

Were I you (Were I in your position), I wouldn't worry about it.

Were it not for weekends, I would go insane.
ただし、次のような定型表現もある
Without weekends, I would go insane. *
But for your help, I couldn't do the work. *
*後には節ではなく名詞的な語句がつづく。

Focal Point 2: 仮定法過去完了：過去の事実に反することを仮定・想像・願望するため、過去完了形を使う。

基本形 If + 主語 + 動詞（過去完了形）〜 , 主語 + would/could/might + 動詞（過去分詞形）

現実： I didn't know you were in the hospital, so I couldn't visit you.
　　　［あなたが入院していることを知らなかった。だから、見舞いに行けなかった］

仮定： If I **had known** you were in the hospital, I **could have visited** you.
　　　［あなたが入院していることを知っていたら、お見舞いに行けたのに］

・仮定法過去を利用した定型表現

If I **had known** you were in the hospital,
I could have visited you.

もし・・・がなかったら

If it **had not been for** your help, I would have failed.［もし君の助けがなかったら、失敗していただろう］

・if がないパターン

Had I **known** you were in the hospital,
I could have visited you.

Had it not been for your help, I would have failed.

Without your help, I would have failed. *
But for your help, I would have failed. *
*後には節ではなく名詞的な語句がつづく。

▶ Exercise I

A. Listen to the recording and complete each sentence.　　🎧 DL 56　◎ CD 56

1. If I (　　　　　) enough time, I (　　　　　　　　　　　　　) today.
2. If I (　　　　　) in charge, I (　　　　　) things differently.
3. (　　　　　) it (　　　　　) all right if I (　　　　　　　　　) to the party tonight?
4. If I (　　　　　　) a hit at that time, our team (　　　　　　) the game.
5. If it (　　　　　　) for your help and advice, we (　　　　　　　) the task.

B. Rewrite the sentence in a different way by starting with "If...".

1. 現在の事実　　　　I **don't have** my smartphone today, so I **cannot call** her now.
   事実と異なる仮定　If _____.

2. 現在の事実　　　　Today **isn't** Saturday, so we **will have to** go to work.
   事実と異なる仮定　If _____.

3. 過去の事実　　　　I **didn't get up** early, so I **couldn't attend** the important lecture.
   事実と異なる仮定　If _____.

4. 過去の事実　　　　Greg **didn't show up** at the party last night, so I **couldn't tell** him the news.
   事実と異なる仮定　If _____.

C. Greg and Ken are talking about Ken's new apartment. Listen to the conversation and choose the best answer to the question.　　🎧 DL 57　◎ CD 57

On which of the following did Ken put special importance?

a. convenience　　　　　　b. rent　　　　c. apartment layout

D. Listen to the conversation again and compare the sentences.

Greg: Ken, when did you move into this apartment?

Ken: About three weeks ago.

Greg: How do you like living here?

Ken: I like it, even though it's a little far from the station. Actually, the real estate agent showed me a different one close to the station. It was very convenient, but the rent was out of my budget. If the rent (1.　　　　　) lower, I (2.　　　　　　　) that apartment.

▶ Basic Phrases in Social Settings

A. 鈴木教授（Professor Suzuki）のレポートの提出締め切りを過ぎてしまったという友達に相談された。

もし私があなただったら、今すぐに鈴木教授に連絡を取るでしょうね。

If I were you, _____

_____ .

---

2. どうして間に合わなかったのかを聞いてみたら、「あのときこうしていれば・・・」と後悔している様子。

あのとき、もっと一生懸命勉強していたら、レポートを書くのに苦労しなかったのになぁ。

If I had studied harder, _____

_____ .

もっと早く出発していたら、電車の遅延に巻き込まれなかったのになぁ。

If I had left earlier, _____

_____ .

あなた自身の言葉で・・・

_____

_____

_____ .

▶ Wrap-Up Writing

If you won one million yen in the lottery, what would you do with it?

Conditionals (2)

Main Points

- should や were to を用いて、万が一の事態や通常では起こり得ない出来事を表すことができる。(仮定法未来)
- wish を使って、「〜すれば[であれば]いいのになぁ」という実現(ほぼ)不可能な願望を述べることができる。

▶ Preparation II

Write or choose a suitable expression for each situation.

1. You are at a piano concert, listening to beautiful piano music. You are impressed with the performance.

   あんな風にピアノが弾けたらなあ。

   I wish _____

   _____ .

2. 保険に入るかどうかを考えながら…。

   万が一、私に何かが起きたら、家族はどうするだろうか

   a. If anything were to happen to me, what would my family do?

   b. If something were happened to me, what would my family do?

   c. If anything should happen to me, what will my family do?.

▶ **Awakening II**

A. Greg is asking Ken for a favor. Listen to their conversation and choose the best answer to each question. 🎧 DL 58 ◎ CD 58

1. How did Ken react to Greg?

   a. Ken declined Greg's request.

   b. Ken proposed a better way to find Carol.

   c. Ken was confused as he did not know Carol.

2. What will Greg most likely do next?

   a. He will wait for Carol's reply to Ken.

   b. He will make a phone call.

   c. He will send a LINE message to Carol.

B. Listen to the conversation again and complete the sentences.

Greg: Hi, Ken, if you (1.   ) into Carol, (2.   ) tell her I'm looking for her?

Ken: Sure. No problem. But don't you have her phone number?

Greg: No. I should have asked her for it.

Ken: I happen to have her LINE ID. Should I send a message to her now?

Greg: Great! Thank you. (3.   ) it!

▶ **Grammar Part II** Conditionals

Focal Point 1: wish を使う仮定法 現在や過去の事実に反することを願望するため、時制をずらす。

①主語 + wish (that) S + 動詞（過去単純形）〜 . ／ could/would + 動詞の原形 〜 .

②主語 + wish (that) S + 動詞（過去完了形）〜 . ／ could have + 動詞の過去分詞形〜 .

① 「〜すれば［であれば］いいのになぁ」という意味を表し、「事実」とは異なる願いを述べます。

   I wish you **were** here. ［あなたがここにいたらなぁ］

   I wish it **would** stop raining. ［雨が止んでくれたらなぁ］

② 「（あの時［その時]）〜した［だった］らよかったのに」という意味を表し、過去の「事実」とは異なる願いを述べます。

   I wish I **hadn't eaten** so much. ［（あのとき）そんなに食べるんじゃなかったなぁ］

   I wish he **could have persuaded** his captain then. ［あのとき彼がキャプテンを説得できていたらなぁ］

Focal Point 2:

仮定法未来　現在・未来において容易に起こりそうもないことを述べる場合で、直接法（仮定法現在）よりも、さらに強い仮想を表します。

基本形①　If ＋ 主語 ＋ **should** ＋ 動詞の原形 〜 , (please) 動詞の原形 … .

　　　　　If ＋ 主語 ＋ **should** ＋ 動詞の原形 〜 , 主語 ＋ **will/would** ＋ 動詞の原形 … .

基本形②　If ＋ 主語 ＋ **were to** ＋ 動詞の原形 〜 , 主語 ＋ **would/could** ＋ 動詞の原形 … .

If the waiter **should come** before I return, please **order** me a coffee.

　［もし万が一ウエイターが私が戻るまえにきたら、コーヒーを注文してください］

If I **were to say** "yes", what **would** you **do**?

　［もし仮に私が「イエス」と言ったら、あなたはどうするつもりですか］

• 仮定法未来を利用した表現例

万が一にも…だったら

If something **should happen**, **call** me.

If I **should become** a millionaire, I **will** live in Hawaii.

あり得ない事だけれど、仮に…だったら

If the sun **were to** rise in the west tomorrow, I **would** marry you.

• if がないパターン

（should が文頭に出る倒置）

Should something **happen**, call me.

Should I **become** a millionaire, I will live in Hawaii.

Were the sun **to rise** in the west tomorrow, I **would** marry you.

▶ **Exercise II**

A. Listen to the recording and complete each sentence.　🎧 DL 59　◎ CD 59

1. I (　　　　　　　) you (　　　　　　　　) here with me today.

2. I (　　　　　　　) you (　　　　　　　　　) me about it when I saw you yesterday.

3. If it (　　　　　　) tomorrow, we (　　　　　　　　　) the picnic.

4. If this (　　　　　　　) your last meal, what (　　　　　　　) you eat?

5. (　　　　　　　　　　) anything, please (　　　　　　　　　　) to contact me.

B. Rewrite the sentences in a different way by using the verb "wish".

1. 現在の事実　　　　I'm sorry I **cannot stay** any longer.
   事実と異なる願望　I wish I _____ .

2. 現在の事実　　　　Ken is sorry his family doesn't live with him.
   事実と異なる願望　Ken wishes _____ .

3. 現在の事実　　　　I'm sorry I'm not tolerant.
   事実と異なる願望　I wish _____ .

4. 過去の事実　　　　I'm sorry I couldn't solve the last question on the test.
   事実と異なる願望　I wish I _____ .

C. Put the Japanese sentences into English by filling in the missing information.

1. もし今日天気が良かったら、私たちはドライブに行けるのに。
   If the weather (　　　　　) good today, we (　　　　　　　　　　　).

2. 時計の針（時間）を戻すことができればなあ。
   (　　　　　　　　　) I could turn back the hands of time.

3. 最悪の事態が万が一起きた場合、あなたはどうしますか。
   If the worst (　　　　　　　), (　　　　　　　　) you do?

4. **A:** 仮に世界のどこでも良いから住める機会をもらったとしたら、あなたはどこに住みたいですか。
   If you (　　　　　　　　) have the chance to live anywhere in the world, (　　　　　　)
   to live.

   B: Well, were I to live abroad, I would live in France.

5. **A:** あのとき私が彼を説得できていたらなぁ。
   I wish (　　　　　　　　　) him at that time.

   B: I know, but you cannot change the past. Let's try our best.

▶ Final Touch

A. Choose a suitable expression for each situation. There may be more than one correct answer.

1. 「明日の運転免許の試験に合格することを願っています」と、友人に言う。
   - (A) I hope you can pass the driving test tomorrow.
   - (B) I wish you can pass the driving test tomorrow.
   - (C) I wish you could pass the driving test tomorrow.

2. 「もし僕だったら、そのコートは買わないなぁ」と、遠回しに彼女に助言する。
   - (A) I think you had better not buy that coat.
   - (B) If I were you, I wouldn't buy that coat.
   - (C) Were I you, I wouldn't buy that coat.

3. 「万が一洗濯機の調子が何か悪い場合は、この番号に電話をしてください」と、洗濯機を設置しに来た人が言う。
   - (A) If there should be something wrong with the washing machine, please call this number.
   - (B) If there were something wrong with the washing machine, please call this number.
   - (C) Should there be something wrong with the washing machine, please call this number.

▶ Wrap-Up Writing

If you could go back to a time and place in the past, when and where would you go? Why? Use specific reasons and details to support your answer.

Grammar Launch
キャリアを拓く総合英語

2020 年 3 月 20 日　初版第 1 刷発行
2024 年 2 月 20 日　初版第 5 刷発行

著　者　　吉原　学
　　　　　中川　知佳子
　　　　　Gregory Ashley

発行者　　福 岡 正 人
発行所　　株式会社　金 星 堂

（〒101-0051）東京都千代田区神田神保町 3-21
Tel. (03) 3263-3828（営業部）
　　 (03) 3263-3997（編集部）
Fax (03) 3263-0716
http://www.kinsei-do.co.jp

編集担当　平田英司　　　　　　　　　　Printed in Japan
印刷所・製本所／株式会社カシヨ
本書の無断複製・複写は著作権法上での例外を除き禁じられています。本書を代行業者等の第三者に依頼してスキャンやデジタル化することは、たとえ個人や家庭内での利用であっても認められておりません。
落丁・乱丁本はお取り替えいたします。

ISBN978-4-7647-4112-6　C1082